The
INTERNATIONAL
CHILI SOCIETY

OFFICIAL
CHILI
COOKBOOK

The INTERNATIONAL CHILI SOCIETY

OFFICIAL CHILI COOKBOOK

by Martina and William Neely

ST. MARTIN'S PRESS • NEW YORK

Copyright © 1981 by Martina and William Neely
For information, write: St. Martin's Press,
175 Fifth Avenue, New York, N.Y. 10010
Manufactured in the United States of America

Design by Manuela Paul
10 9 8 7 6 5 4 3 2

Neely, Martina.
The International Chili Society official chili cookbook.

1. Chili con carne. I. Neely, Bill, joint author.
II. International Chili Society.
III. Title.
TX749.N4   641.8'2   80-29054
ISBN 0-312-41988-0

To Walter Neely, III

Acknowledgements

In our travels throughout the United States we learned, to our delight, just how important chili is to people everywhere. We found chili cookoffs in the North woods and chili parlors throughout the South and Southwest, many dating back to the turn of the century. And everywhere we went, we found people willing to give us the local chili recipes, or to help us find authentic ones. It is to these people, organizations, and companies who were so helpful that we offer a hearty "thank you." The book would not have been the same without you. In fact, there would have been no book. And a special note of gratitude goes to Carroll Shelby, whose idea the book was in the first place. We would also like to thank the following: Department of Horticulture, New Mexico State University, Cooperative Extension Service, New Mexico State University, Jeanne Croft, New Mexico State University, Dr. Roy M. Nakayama, New Mexico State University, American Spice Trade Association, The McIlhenny Company (Tabasco), Institute of Texan Cultures, Lynda Katonak, *Holiday* magazine, Heublein Grocery Products Division, San Antonio Historical Society, The Balboa Bay Club, Montezuma Tequila, division Barton Brands, Hillbilly Chili Society, Chilli Man Chilli Mix, Joe DeFrates, Pepsico Goat Gap Gazette, Anheuser-Busch, International Connoisseurs of Green and Red Chile, Cal-Compack Foods, Inc., *Roanoke Times & World News,* and *The New York Times.*

In addition we thank the following people and chapters of the International Chili Society: Jim West, Bill Ray, C. V. Wood, Jr., Ormly Gumfudgin, Bill Neale and Pancho McNiff; West Virginia, Virginia, Arizona,

Colorado, New Mexico, Michigan, Oklahoma, Lower Colorado, Georgia, and Apple Valley Chapters.

If, in our enthusiasm to get this to the publisher, we have overlooked anybody, please forgive us. It was certainly not intentional, and we did appreciate your help.

Contents

Somewhere Along the Trail
–A History of Chili

From the time the second person on earth mixed some chile peppers with meat and cooked them, the great chili debate was on; more of a war, in fact. The desire to brew up the best bowl of chili in the world is exactly that old.

Perhaps it is the effect of *Capsicum* spices upon man's mind; for, in the immortal words of Joe DeFrates, the only man ever to win the National *and* the World Chili Championships, "Chili powder makes you crazy." That may say it all. To keep things straight, *chile* refers to the pepper pod, and *chili* to the concoction. The *e* and the *i* of it all.

The great debate, it seems, is not limited to whose chili is *best*. Even more heated is the argument over *where* the first bowl was made; and by *whom*. Estimates range from "somewhere west of Laramie," in the early nineteenth century—being a product of a Texas trail drive—to a grisly tale of enraged Aztecs, who cut up invading Spanish conquistadores, seasoned chunks of them with a passel of chile peppers, and ate them.

Never has there been anything mild about chili.

Our travels through Texas, New Mexico, and California, and even Mexico, over the years have failed to turn up the elusive "best bowl of chili." Every state lays claim to the title, and certainly no Texan worth his *comino* (cumin) would think, even for a moment, that it rests anywhere else but in the Lone Star State—and probably right in his own blackened and battered chili pot.

There may not be an answer. There are, however, certain facts that one cannot overlook. The mixture of meat, beans, peppers, and herbs was known to the Incas, Aztecs, and Mayan Indians long before Columbus and the conquistadores.

Fact: Chile peppers were used in Cervantes's Spain and show up in great ancient cuisines of China, India, Indonesia, Italy, the Caribbean, France, and the Arab states.

Fact: Don Juan de Oñate entered what is now New Mexico in 1598 and brought with him the green chile pepper. It has grown there for the nearly four hundred years since.

Fact: Canary Islanders, transplanted in San Antonio as early as 1723, used local peppers, wild onions, garlic, and other spices to concoct pungent meat dishes—improvising upon ones they had cooked for generations in their native land, where the chile pepper also grew.

Exit fact, enter conjecture.

There is little doubt that cattle drovers and trail hands did more to popularize the dish throughout the Southwest than anybody else, and there is a tale that we heard one frosty night in a Texican bar in Marfa, Texas, about a range cook who made chili along all the great cattle trails of Texas. He collected wild oregano, chile peppers, wild garlic, and onions and mixed it all with the fresh-killed beef or buffalo—or jackrabbit, armadillo, rattlesnake, or whatever he had at hand—and the cowhands ate it like ambrosia. And to make sure he had an ample supply of native spices wherever he went, he planted gardens along the paths of the cattle drives—mostly in patches of mesquite—to protect them from the hooves of the marauding cattle. The next time the drive went by there, he found his garden and harvested the crop, hanging the peppers and onions and oregano to dry on the side of the chuck wagon. The cook blazed a trail across Texas with tiny, spicy gardens.

As cattle trail chili grew in popularity throughout the tiny Texas trail towns, so, too, did its devotees. Frank and Jesse James fell prey to its taste and are said to have eaten a few bowls of "red" before pulling many of their bank jobs. At least one town, it is noted, was spared from their shooting and looting by the local chili parlor. Fort Worth had a chili joint just north of town, and the James boys rode in there *just for the chili,* vowing never to rob their bank because "anyplace that has a chili joint like this just oughta' be treated better."

And Pat Garrett is supposed to have said of William Bonney—Billy the Kid: "Anybody that eats chili can't be all bad."

Chili cooks are probably as creative with their stories as they are with their broth, but what can you expect when you go through Texas asking questions about chili? It's the home of the tall tale.

In case you ever want to brew up a batch of "original Texas chili," here is a version we got that night in Marfa—well, at least, a composite from a few of the old-timers at the bar; their account of what they remember the first recipe to be. There is a little of the influence of each side of the Rio Grande because there was a mixture there, and if you get right down to it, that probably describes the heritage of chili about as well as anything. This "original" recipe may be traced back to that same range cook who planted his gardens across Texas in the early 1800s. And it may well have been the granddaddy of the blend that Frank and Jesse were addicted to.

Nobody will swear that it was the first true Texas chili recipe, but they all say it was close to it:

Chile Con Carne

Cut up as much meat as you think you will need (any kind will do, but beef is probably best) in pieces about the size of a pecan. Put it in a pot, along with some suet (enough so as the meat won't stick to the sides of the pot), and cook it with about the same amount of wild onions, garlic, oregano, and chiles as you have got meat. Put in some salt. Stir it from time to time and cook it until the meat is as tender as you think it's going to get.

The entire chili exercise, at that point in history, was undoubtedly out of necessity. If you have ever tasted fresh-killed beef, you know how much a lot of spices would help the flavor. The range cooks, too, knew this. They also knew the cowpokes would have strung them up right on the spot for serving plain beef in that unaged state. There also is no question that the spices helped preserve the meat and often masked the flavor of meat that was near spoiling; so the trail cook frequently brewed up *chile con carne*, which is simply the Spanish way of saying "peppers and meat." The name, incidentally, is as close as any self-respecting Mexican cares to get in claiming the dish's place of origin.

By the time we had finished writing down the recipe, the number of Tex-Mex patrons in the tiny bar had grown considerably, and each had his own version of cattle drive chili stories—each one becoming more embellished as the *cerveza* flowed. Then one hauled out a yellowed clipping from his wallet. He didn't remember what newspaper it had come from, or even when. He just knew he had had it a long time. It was a prayer—something an old, black range cook had prayed once. His name, euphonically, was Bones Hooks, and the prayer went:

> Lord, God, you know us old cowhands is forgetful. Sometimes, I can't even recollect what happened yesterday. We is forgetful. We just know daylight from dark, summer, fall, winter, and spring. But I sure hope we don't never forget to thank you before we eat a mess of good chili.
>
> We don't know why, in your wisdom, you been so doggone good to us. The heathen Chinese don't have no chili, never. The Frenchmen is left out. The Russians don't know no more about chili than a hog knows about a sidesaddle. Even the Mexicans don't get a good whiff of chili unless they live around here.
>
> Chili-eaters is some of your chosen people, Lord. We don't know why you're so doggone good to us. But, Lord God, don't never think we ain't grateful for this chili we are about to eat. Amen.

Chili buffs in San Antonio—and in most of Texas, for that matter—say the stuff called "chili" was invented there, probably by "Chili Queens," women who dotted the Military Plaza and sold highly seasoned brews called "chili" from rudimentary carts, all through the night, to a cadre of customers who rode in from all over the prairies to singe their tonsils. The "Queens" did exist, for nearly two hundred years, the locals say. Yet most historians fail to tell of them selling chili much before 1880. Before then it was probably strictly Mexican food.

If chili next moved from the greatly romanticized cattle trail to the Military Plaza at San Antonio, it also moved right back into the factual stage. It is all pretty well documented from there. The "Queens" may have been there for two hundred years, but they probably had sold chili only for the last third of that period; and, if for no other reason than one that usually improves a product, they began to refine and add sophistication to the dish. They brought it somewhere near today's stage. The reason, of course, was competition. There were dozens of the Chili Queens on the plaza, and you can bet that each one was constantly striving to improve her blend, simply to attract more customers than any of the competition.

The Queens, who were for the most part Mexican, made their chili at home and then loaded it onto colorful little chili wagons, on which they transported it to the plaza, along with pots, crockery, and all the other gear necessary to feed the nineteenth-century night people. They built mesquite fires on the square to keep the chili warm, lighted the wagons with colored lanterns, and squatted on the ground beside the cart, dishing out chili to customers who sat on wooden stools to eat the delightful and fiery stew.

All this went on from nightfall until just before sunrise, when the vegetable vendors came on with their carts to occupy the Military Plaza, which had become known as "La Plaza del Chile con Carne."

The Chili Queens remained a highlight in San Antonio for many years (there was even a "San Antonio Chili Stand" at the Chicago World's Fair in 1893), until the late 1930s, in fact, when the health department put an end to their time-honored profession.

The following is reprinted from the *San Antonio Light* of September 12, 1937:

Recent action of the city health department in ordering removal from Haymarket square of the chili queens and their stands brought an end to a 200-year-old tradition.

The chili queens made their first appearance a couple of centuries back after a group of Spanish soldiers camped on what is now the city hall site and gave the place the name, Military Plaza.

At one time the chili queens had stands on Military,

Haymarket and Alamo plazas but years ago the city confined them to Haymarket plaza.

According to Tax Commissioner Frank Bushick, a contemporary and a historian of those times, the greatest of all the queens was no Mexican but an American named Sadie. Another famous queen was a senorita named Martha who later went on the stage.

Writing men like Stephen Crane and O. Henry were impressed enough to immortalize the queens in their writings.

With the disappearance from the plaza of the chili stands, the troubadors who roamed the plaza for years also have disappeared into the night.

Some of the chili queens have simply gone out of business. Others, like Mrs. Eufemia Lopez and her daughters, Juanita and Esperanza Garcia, have opened indoor cafes elsewhere.

But henceforth the San Antonio visitor must forego his dining on chili al fresco.

From the research library of the Institute of Texan Cultures comes this link with the past—a Chili Queen recipe (slightly updated for shopping convenience):

===

Original San Antonio Chili

2 pounds beef shoulder, cut into ½-inch cubes
1 pound pork shoulder, cut into ½-inch cubes
¼ cup suet
¼ cup pork fat
3 medium-sized onions, chopped
6 garlic cloves, minced
1 quart water
4 ancho chiles

1 serrano chile
6 dried red chiles
1 tablespoon *comino* seeds, freshly ground
2 tablespoons Mexican oregano
Salt to taste

Place lightly floured beef and pork cubes in with suet and pork fat in heavy chili pot and cook quickly, stirring often. Add onions and garlic and cook until they are tender and limp. Add water to mixture and simmer slowly while preparing chiles. Remove stems and seeds from chiles and chop very finely. Grind chiles in *molcajete* (mortar and pestle). After meat, onion, and garlic has simmered about 1 hour, add chiles. Grind comino seeds in *molcajete* and add oregano with salt to mixture. Simmer another 2 hours. Remove suet casing and skim off some fat. Never cook frijoles with chiles and meat. Serve as separate dish.

The hearty smell of mesquite smoke mingling with the spicy aroma of chiles is gone. Gone, too, are the gaily painted carts and the fancy costumes and flowers of the Chili Queens. But before their passing, chili had become somewhat of a national dish.

Chili parlors sprang up all over the country, and many small-town cafés served little else than chili. By the depression years, there was hardly a town that didn't have a chili parlor, even if it was nothing more than a hole-in-the-wall place with half-a-dozen bar stools in front of a linoleum-topped counter. To many a wandering work-seeker in those depression days, the wayside chili shack meant the difference between starvation and staying alive. Chili was cheap and crackers were free.

Joe DeFrates's father, "Port," worked as a bartender at the Adolphis Hotel in Dallas in 1914 and learned to love the chili that was served in the chili parlor just off the main lobby of the lavish hotel. When the older DeFrates returned to his native Springfield, Illinois, to open his own place, serving chili only to his friends and regular customers (it was not on the menu), he found chili parlors everywhere. He also found that the name of the dish was spelled *chilli*, because a sign painter named Sheehan had made an error when lettering the window of a local chili parlor and everybody liked it so much that it stayed. To this day, it is spelled with two *l*s in Illinois.

By the fifties, everybody was talking and writing about chili. Columnist Westbrook Pegler was taken to task by chili lovers everywhere when he suggested that chili should be made with beans. In response to the flood of mail, Pegler wrote:

> In praising the beautiful version of chili-con that was revealed to me in my gallivanting youth in the Mid and Southwest I had no intention to invite or wage controversy. Yet I should have remembered that gladsomeness begets its own comeuppance and that compliments are made only on pain of angry dissent.
>
> During his Christmas trip home President Truman stopped at Vergne Dixon's chili parlor at 1904–06 Olive St., Kansas City, and put himself outside a bowl of chili along with a scuttle of beer fetched him from yonder, Mr. Dixon having no beer license.
>
> It seems to me that some law got busted here, but I am not for multiplying our President's problems, so I will only mutter in a low voice that the W.C.T.U., which hollered murder when our troops got beer in Korea, certainly booted one.
>
> I am afraid I carried on when I got going about chili-con, for this delicatessen is downright spiritual with us who long since sat on the high stools, as Mr. Truman did in Dixon's, and on $25 a week got by payday to payday, well-fed and well-content.
>
> I wrote that chili-con should be made with ground beef, beans, chili powder, tomatoes, onions and garlic, and seized an occasion to extol by name the put-up chili and the beans and powder sold by Gebhardt's of El Paso.

I had no inkling of the feeling among the devotees of the house of Gebhardt, who fell on me in numbers, by telegram and mail.

Not only is Gebhardt's an ancient and honorable institution in San Antonio, but Gebhardt's meat is not ground but cooked so well that it comes undone, releasing its juices among the beans. Then, too, I ran afoul of the devotees of Wolf's chili-con and related products, which actually are made in El Paso.

Chili had made it.

In 1952, a Texas journalist who had devoted much of his life to the study of chili wrote a book entitled *With or Without Beans*. His name was Joe Cooper. After examining the best chili on record to that date, he released his own recipe—one that he described as "maybe not the best ever, but one which satisfies the Coopers' appetites," and is one which poses no undue problems for the average home cook. It will put good chili on the table without much effort or attention other than what is normal routine in any kitchen.

Joe Cooper's Chili

3 pounds lean beef (never veal)
¼ cup olive oil
1 quart water
2 bay leaves (if desired)
8 dry chile pods *or*
   6 tablespoons chili powder
3 tablespoons salt
10 cloves finely chopped garlic
1 teaspoon cumin powder
1 teaspoon oregano or marjoram

1 teaspoon red pepper
½ teaspoon black pepper
1 tablespoon sugar
3 tablespoons paprika
3 tablespoons flour
6 tablespoons cornmeal

When olive oil is hot, in 6-quart pot, add meat and sear over high heat; stir constantly until gray—not brown. It then will have consistency of whole-grain hominy. Add 1 quart water and cook (covered) at bubbling simmer 1½ to 2 hours. Then add all ingredients, except flour and cornmeal. Cook another 30 minutes at same bubbling simmer, but no longer, as further cooking will damage some of the spice flavors. Now add thickening, previously mixed in 3 tablespoons cold water. Cook 5 minutes to determine if more water is necessary (likely) for your desired consistency. Stir to prevent sticking after thickening is added. Some prefer all flour, others all cornmeal, and still others use cracker meal—about as good, and more convenient. Suit your own taste.

Some Texans agree with Joe Cooper, some don't. Hal John Wimberly, editor and publisher of the *Goat Gap Gazette,* a Houston newspaper "mainly for chiliheads and their ilk," likes it simple. He says reverently of chili: "I don't know why people screw around with it. It's a marvelous dish if you treat it right, with a few simple ingredients. I mean, look at California cooks, they're likely to throw the whole garden in."

Wimberly brings to light yet another controversy that has raged among chili cooks since the beginning of time: whether or not one should put tomatoes in chili. "Jailhouse chili," he says, "is a good example. It's always been a favorite. It has been served to many a prisoner, and it was always very basic—meat, spices, peppers, and grease from the suet."

Over the past one hundred fifty years, many personalities and anecdotes have been linked with chili. It has been lauded by presidents, show-business types have defended it, and it was said that Will Rogers judged a town by its chili, and even kept scores.

Chili aficionados are no longer mostly Texans. The famous Chasen's restaurant in Beverly Hills serves more "Soup of the Devil" to international celebrities than any other restaurant. Jack Benny, J. Edgar Hoover, and even Elizabeth Taylor have eaten chili there. In fact, Liz had some Chasen's chili sent, frozen, to her in Rome during the shooting of *Cleopatra*.

Frank Tolbert, the noted Texas chili authority, received 29,000 letters from all over the world relating chili experiences after an article of his appeared in the *Saturday Evening Post*.

In 1977, a bill was introduced in the Texas legislature to designate chili as the official state dish, and one year earlier, back in California, Rufus (Rudy) Valdez, a full-blooded Ute Indian, won the world chili championship, using what he claimed to be a two thousand-year-old recipe.

"Originally," says Valdez, "chili was made with meat of horses or deer, chile peppers and cornmeal from ears of stalks that grew only to the knee. No beans." Valdez says he got his recipe from his grandmother when he was a boy on the Ute reservation near Ignacio, Colorado. She lived to the age of 102 and Valdez says she credited her longevity and that of her relatives to the powers of chili. Actually, he says, chili was invented by the Pueblo cliff dwellers in Mesa Verde who passed it on to the Navajos before it became popular with the Utes.

Carroll Shelby is more sanguine in his approach: "The beauty of chili to me is that it's really a state of mind," he says. "It's what you want when you make it. You can put anything in there you want, make it hot or mild, any blend of spices you feel like at the time. You make it up to suit your mood."

So the chili pot still boils. As does the controversy. We certainly don't know who started it, or where. We just know that, as with Billy the Kid, anybody who likes chili can't be all bad.

A Spicy Past –A History of the Chile Pepper

It was only a quirk of history that gave Peter Piper the chance to pick a peck of pickled peppers. What he picked should never have been called peppers.

The error occurred when the early Spanish explorers came to the Caribbean. Bear in mind that they were looking for a shorter water route to the spice riches of the East. And, even in those days, pepper—true pepper—was the most valuable spice.

In the islands of the New World they found little red vegetable pods, which the Indians used in cooking and which imparted a sharp bite to food. In what may have been innocent confusion, or perhaps a little face-saving, the Spaniards named this discovery *pepper*. Technically, these pod-bearing plants are known as *Capsicums*.

14

Though there is no botanical relationship between the *Capsicum* pods of the Western world and the true pepper berries (peppercorns) of the East, the misnomer *pepper* has stuck with the red pods (of Peter Piper fame) down through the centuries.

Adding to the confusion, the red podded *Capsicum* family proved to be extremely adaptable when the explorers sent seeds back to Europe. In an amazingly short time, the cultivation of *Capsicum* pods spread to almost every part of the world. Moreover, in many places the pods developed different characteristics as to shape, color, size, and pungency. Before long the *Capsicum* family grew into one of the largest and most diversified clans in the plant world and the term *pepper* became all the more misunderstood.

The term *Capsicum* is a genus name encompassing five species and some three hundred different varieties of plants producing fleshy, vegetable pods. Botanically, it is part of the *Solanaceae* or nightshade family, which also gives us tomatoes and tobacco.

In consumer terms, the *Capsicum* family gives us paprika, red pepper (including "cayenne"), chile pepper, chili powder, and sweet (or bell) pepper flakes. *Capsicum* can also be found in many spice blends such as barbecue spice, seasoning salt, meat tenderizers, taco seasonings, and others. Hot pepper sauce in its many forms just couldn't be made without *Capsicum*.

The property that separates the *Capsicum* family from other plant groups is *capsaicin,* a crystalline substance that is extremely pungent. The higher the *capsaicin* content, the hotter the pepper. All *Capsicums* have some *capsaicin,* but in such varieties as the sweet bell peppers it has been so minimized through cultivation over the years that the flavor today imparts little or no tang. The same is true for the mild, sweet types of paprika and especially those strains developed by producers in the United States.

The chile pepper is native to the Americas, growing as a wild perennial from South America north into Mexico and southern Texas. It was cultivated by prehistoric Indians and has been established as a main nutritional source of the Indians in Peru in 4000 B.C. A chronicler of the Cortez expedition of 1529 wrote that "Montezuma was accustomed to eat a light breakfast of chile peppers and nothing else."

In ancient Peru, the pungent pod was called *aji* pronounced "ah-hee," which is invariably what everyone said upon first taste. As *aji* was carried north, the name was translated into colloquial Spanish and became known as "chile."

From the time Don Juan de Oñate, a Spanish explorer, entered New Mexico in 1598, the Southwest's history has been laced with chiles.

In 1889, Emilil Ortega, an early meat-packer, traveled from California to New Mexico to study alfalfa and beef production in the area. While in New Mexico, he happened to take dinner with a friend and was introduced to chile. By the time he left New Mexico, in 1895, he realized the value of the pungent pepper and took enough seeds with him to begin growing his own.

By 1890 a German immigrant, Willie Gebhardt, had developed a chili powder by grinding chiles and blending them with other spices. In 1896, he opened a small plant in New Braunfels, Texas, to sell his new product. Two years later he moved the whole operation to San Antonio, Texas, and the company has been in business there ever since, using exactly the same secret formula.

While Gebhardt was making chili powder in Texas, Ortega had planted his first crop of chile in Ventura, California. For five long years, he patiently carried water from the river to irrigate his crops. In 1900 he went into commercial production of chile, and in 1902, the Musser Seed Co. offered a California chile seed, which is believed to have been developed by Ortega between 1895 and 1900. (Ortega married twice and had his last child at the age of seventy-three. His brother won his last rodeo contest at the age of seventy. It seems fair to assume that their longevity and productivity can be attributed, in part, to the pungent pods produced from the chile seeds carried from the "Land of Enchantment.")

In 1907, Dr. Fabian Garcia, at the New Mexico State University Agricultural Experiment Station, began working to improve the varieties of chile grown in New Mexico. In 1908, Dr. Garcia noted that chile was being canned in Los Angeles, California, and in Las Cruces, New Mexico.

Since 1908, there have been numerous companies entering the chile processing business, and the market for chile products and Mexican foods has expanded throughout the world.

Dr. Roy Minoru Nakayama, noted chile horticulturist better known as "Mr. Chile," might sit back and reflect on the contributions he has made to the enjoyment of mankind if he weren't so busy trying to develop new varieties of the precious pod!

In 1975, Dr. Nakayama released a new chile variety that seemed to be the processor's dream: It was hearty, pungent, and huge. Named in honor of a local farmer, Jim Lytle, who had worked closely with Dr. Nakayama in his chile experiments, *Numex Big Jim* sparked the imagination of chile lovers everywhere—just thinking about a foot-long, five-ounce chile set tongues wagging and watering!

New Mexico State has received numerous requests for ways to identify the different varieties of chile. With Dr. Nakayama's help, we are able to identify and describe the eighteen most commonly used chiles:

NUMEX BIG JIM: Long, green, thick flesh pod, medium pungent. Average length: 7¾", 1¾–2" wide, with slightly flattened pods. Used mainly for canning and freezing.

NMSU EXPERIMENTAL: Long, green processing type. Mild pungency with thick pod flesh. Pods average 6½–7″ long, 1¾″ wide, and are slightly flattened. Used green for canning and freezing; red for mild powder.

MIRASOL: Small, elongated type with pungent pods. Average 2½–3″ long, ½–¾″ wide, with medium flesh thickness. Used for making hot salsa.

ANCHO: Short, wide pod type. Varies from mild to medium pungency (depending on seed source). Average 3–4″ long, 2–3″ wide, dark emerald green to dark reddish brown and wrinkled pod surface when dry. Medium flesh thickness.

JALAPEÑO: Short pod type. Pungent with cylindrical shape. Pods average 2″ long and are ¾–1″ wide, dark green color with some pods having longitudinal scars on the surface. Used for canning whole, pickling, and hot salsa.

MEXICAN IMPROVED: Medium long, very pungent. Pods average 3″ long, 2″ wide, and are slightly flattened with wide shoulders, uniformly tapering to the point. Medium flesh thickness. Used green for hot salsa, red for hot powder.

SERRANO: Small pod type, very pungent. Pods 1–1½″ long, ⅜″ wide. Medium pod flesh thickness, dark green color. Used green for pickling and hot salsa.

HOT CHERRY: Small globose pod type. Very pungent. Pods 1–1½″ in diameter, thick pod flesh. Used green for pickling and hot salsa.

SANTAKA: Small pod type, very pungent pods. Average 2″ long, ⅜″ diameter, with medium pod flesh thickness. Used green for hot salsa, red for hot chili powder.

FRESNO: Small pod type. Pungent with medium thick pod flesh, slightly wider at calyx end, gradually tapering to a point. Pods 6½–7″ long, 1¾″ in diameter. Light green to greenish in color. Used for hot salsa and pickling.

SANDIA: Long green type. Pungent with medium thick pod flesh, slightly wider at calyx end, gradually tapering to a point. Pods 6½–7″ long, 1¾″ in diameter, with slightly roughened pod appearance. Used for processing as hot green; red as hot whole pods or as hot powder.

TABASCO: Very small pod type. Very pungent with medium pod thickness. Pods 1–1½″ long, ½–⅜″ diameter and are a light yellow color. Used green for pickling or hot salsa, red for Tabasco sauce.

BAHAMIAN: Very small pod type. Very, very pungent with thin flesh, ¾″ long, ⅛–³⁄₁₆″ in diameter. Used for hot salsa or very hot red powder.

NEW MEXICO NO. 6: Long green pod type, also referred to as New Mexico 6–4. Pod size averages 6–6½″ long, 1¾″ wide, flattened, uniform width almost to tip. Thick pod flesh, smooth skin. Used green for canning and freezing, red for mild powder.

SPANISH PAPRIKA: Round pod type. Not pungent. Pods average 1–1¼″ long, 1½″ wide, and have thin pod flesh. *No green use!* Used red for paprika powder.

CAYENNE: Long pod type. Pungent pods average 6–8″ long, ¾–1″ in diameter, slightly curled rough surface. Thin pod flesh thickness. Limited use as green; used red for hot salsa.

ANAHEIM: Long green type; mild when grown in coastal areas of California, pungent when grown in New Mexico. Pods average 6–7″ long, 1¾″ diameter (California); 6–7″ long, 1¼″ diameter (New Mexico). Canned as mild green in California and used for hot red powder in New Mexico.

BULGARIAN PAPRIKA: Short pod type. Not pungent, medium flesh pod thickness. Pods 2½″ long, 1½″ wide; slightly wider at calyx end. No green use, red for paprika powder.

BASIC SPICES FOR CHILI COOKERY

BASIL   Dried or fresh, the flavor is reminiscent of mint and cloves combined. It is good in almost any dish containing tomatoes, since it seems to sweeten them.

BAY LEAF   Dried or fresh, used sparingly, it is quite strong. The aromatic and slightly bitter flavor enhances meats, fish, poultry, soups, and sauces.

CAYENNE   is a member of the *Capsicum* family. The pepper is ground, mixed with yeast and flour, and baked into a hard cake. After regrinding, it appears on your grocery shelf as a super spice.

CILANTRO   Dried or fresh, it is a great flavor enhancer in Mexican and Chinese cooking. Cilantro is the parsley-like leaf of fresh coriander.

CORIANDER   seeds when dried have a sweet taste reminiscent of lemon peel and sage combined.

CUMIN   seed is similar to caraway seed in flavor and appearance; however it is lighter in color and the flavor is stronger and less refined. Also comes in powdered form.

GARLIC   is one of the most common spices, included in almost every recipe, except ice cream. Garlic—either fresh cloves, powder, or salt—is a necessity to the chili chef.

OREGANO   is a wild marjoram whose taste is sharper and spicier than marjoram's. It is a common ingredient in Spanish and Mexican foods.

PAPRIKA   is a mild, powdered seasoning made from sweet red peppers. Used extensively as a flavor- and color-enhancing additive.

The World Championship Chili Cookoffs and the Story That Started It All

The gastric phenomenon known as the World Championship Chili Cookoff actually got its start with H. Allen Smith's expository article in the August 1967 issue of *Holiday* magazine. Entitled "Nobody Knows More About Chili Than I Do," it was a tongue-in-cheek article about what a fine, upstanding, qualified, high-grade, exceptional chili cook Allen was, while taking the Texans to task for thinking they were the chili experts of the world.

Carroll Shelby's cronies in Dallas called him in from California for a special consultation on how best to handle the fact that chili—Texas style—was being maligned by a rank outsider.

The Texans got together and connived to get Allen to appear on the already sagging front porch of Terlingua's old Chisos Oasis Saloon.

The small but insignificant town of Terlingua is just outside Big Bend National Park in Brewster County, Texas. Located 80.3 miles south of Alpine, Terlingua was once the mercury mining capital of the world, having had a population of two thousand in the 1880s. Before you could say "Chiricahua Ranch," Allen found himself in Terlingua, Texas (population 2), defending his honor at the First Original World's Championship Chili Cookoff, which took place on October 21, 1967.

Allen's most worthy opponent was Wick Fowler, an Austin newspaperman, who flew the banner of the sponsor, The Chili Appreciation Society, International (CASI), and was their official chef.

In its original concept, there was to be one cookoff and only one, for the sole purpose of putting author/humorist Smith in his place. It was well-calculated to be a "put-on" for a "put-down" for whoever could "put up" with it. This dastardly event was created by publicist Tom Tierney and engineered by fellow CASI members (Dave Witts, Bill Neale, and Frank X. Tolbert) in Dallas, with the able assistance of a displaced but fun-loving Texan from California by the name of Carroll Shelby. At that time, Shelby and Dave Witts shared ownership in a large ranch, Chiricahua, which just happened to include the town of Terlingua, which is now a ghost town.

The two chili cooks proceeded to do their thing on the porch in front of a crowd of five hundred beer-drinking chiliheads.

At judging time, the three judges were blindfolded to taste the chili. Hallie Stilwell, justice of the peace, voted for author H. Allen Smith, while Floyd Schneider, of San Antonio, voted for Wick Fowler. Dallas lawyer Dave Witts, mayor of Terlingua, unceremoniously spat out both samples and took the microphone to say: "Ladies and gentlemen, I hereby declare a tie, since my taste buds have been seared and singed, preventing any possibility of a decision at this point in time. I am now declaring a moratorium on this contest . . . until we meet again next year at the same time here in Terlingua, Texas, for the next great Chili Cookoff."

Having mentioned that this was to be the one and only cookoff, at the very last minute, holding the final and decisive vote, Dave realized what a great party-cookoff-outing it had been, and that it should really be done one more time. It was that executive decision, made in just a couple of seconds, that really lit the fuse under thousands of chili pots in the many nationwide cookoffs to follow.

From that humble beginning grew the International Chili Society and its World Championship Chili Cookoff, which draws more than thirty thousand spectators each year to California, where it is now held. Many of the original Texans stayed behind to stage a similar event annually in Terlingua. So, if nothing else, Smith's *Holiday* magazine story started one of the fiercest wars man has known.

"Nobody Knows More About Chili Than I Do"
By H. Allen Smith

When I was a boy of ten in Decatur, Illinois, my mother gave me twenty cents every morning, half of it for carfare to school, the remaining dime for my lunch. I could have spent that dime on candy or ice cream, but I can't recall that I ever did, because it was at this magic and benign moment in time that I discovered chili.

Day after day I went to Chili Bill's joint a couple of blocks from the school, sat at a scrubbed wooden counter, and for my ten cents got a bowl of steaming chili, six soda crackers, and a glass of milk. That was livin'!

I have been a chili man ever since those days. Nay, I have been *the* chili man. Without chili I believe I would wither and die. I stand without a peer as a maker of chili, and as a judge of chili made by other people. No living man, and let us not even think of woman in this connection, *no living man,* I repeat, can put together a pot of chili as ambrosial, as delicately and zestfully flavorful, as the chili I make. This is a fact so stern, so granitic, that it belongs in the encyclopedias, as well as in all standard histories of civilization.

That is the way of us chili men. Each of us knows that *his* chili is light-years beyond other chili in quality and singularity; each of us knows that all other chili is such vile slop that a coyote would turn his back on it.

My brother Sam believes that he should be given the Nobel prize for chili-making. He and I didn't speak for a year and a half because of our clash of views on chili-making. Word got to me that Sam was telling people that our pop had called him the greatest chili-maker in all Christendom. I knew this to be a falsehood; my father had said that *I* was the greatest. My sister Lou tried to deescalate our feud by saying that pop actually had remarked that *he* was the greatest chili-maker in the civilized world.

Brother Sam has gone along for years making chili without so much as a whiff of cumin seed in it, and cumin seed is as essential to chili as meat is to hamburger. I was at Sam's house once and in a moment of fraternal feeling ate a spoonful of his foul chili. I remarked helpfully that it had no cumin seed in it, and Sam said that I could leave his fireside and never come back. "One bowl of your chili," said I, "would pollute the waters of the Great Salt Lake." And off I stomped.

Thus began the feud, and it came to an end only after news reached me that Sam was warring on another chili front. He and I both believe that proper chili should be soupy, with lots of broth. He has a friend named VanPelt who composes thickened chili, Texas style. My chili and Sam's chili are eaten with a soup spoon;

VanPelt eats his from a plate with a fork. Sam and VanPelt broke off relations for a while after a highly seasoned argument over thin versus thick. VanPelt contended that Sam's chili should be eaten through a straw, and Sam said that VanPelt's lavalike chili could be molded into balls and used to hold down tent flaps in a high wind. I was proud of my brother after that; he stood firm against the wretched sort of chili that is eaten from a plate with a fork.

I voted for LBJ in 1964, but I now renounce that vote, for I didn't know of his evil ways with chili. Down on the Pedernales, the President has his chili put together by Mrs. Zephyr Wright or that piebald old character Walter Jetton, who spends his time at the ranch barbecuing up a storm and talking in an ignorant fashion about chili. Miz Wright serves chili *without beans*. Walter Jetton has two recipes: in one he ignores beans, in the other he adds beans and thickens things with cracker meal. There's an old Texas saying that originated in the cow camps, concerning any range cook whose grub was consistently miserable. Of him the cowhands would grumble, "He ain't fit to tote guts to a bear." That, precisely, is what I say of Mr. Cracker Meal Jetton.

You may suspect, by now, that the chief ingredients of all chili are fiery envy, scalding jealousy, scorching contempt, and sizzling scorn. The quarreling that has gone on for generations over New England clam chowder versus Manhattan clam chowder (the Maine legislature once passed a bill outlawing the mixing of tomatoes with clams) is but a minor spat alongside the raging feuds that have arisen out of chili recipes.

A fact so positive as the fact that chili was invented by Texans will, by the very nature of its adamantine unshakability, get shook. Lately it has become fashionable to say chili—contrary to all popular belief—was first devised by Mexicans and then appropriated by the

Texans. Some of the newer cookbooks come right out and say that chili is the national dish of Mexico. In Elena Zelayeta's *Secrets of Mexican Cooking* it is asserted that the popular Mexican dish, *Carne en Salsa de Chile Colorado*—meat in red chile sauce—is much the same as the chili con carne of Texas. "It is a famous Mexican dish," says Señora Zelayeta, "that has been taken and made famous by the Lone Star State." This lady, one of the most respected of contemporary authorities on Mexican cuisine, then proceeds to destroy every shred of her authority by suggesting that a can of hominy goes well in a pot of chili.

On the other hand, if there is any doubt about what the generality of Mexicans think about chili, the *Diccionario de Mejicanismos,* published in 1959, defines chile con carne as "detestable food passing itself off as Mexican, sold in the U.S. from Texas to New York." The Mexicans in turn get told off in a 14th Century English *Herball, or General Historie of Plantes,* in which is written of the chile pepper: "It killeth dogs."

I am a frequent visitor in Mexico, and once, in a sportive mood, I decided to introduce chili into Mexico, get the Mexicans to making it in their homes and setting up chili joints along the highways. I have a good friend, once a novice bullfighter that failed at that trade, who is maitre d'hotel of a large restaurant. When he found out what I was doing, he spoke to me in soft and liquid accents: "If I ever hear you spick the words of chili con carne one more time in our beloved raypooblica, *pues,* I am not in the custom of spitting in the eye of gringos, but I will spit in your eye with glory and speed and hardness." He didn't make it with the bulls but I felt that he could make it with me, and so I gave up the chili-con-carnization of Mexico.

One present-day dabbler in chili lore has come up with a shocking discovery which he believes is proof that chili con carne had its origin in Mexico. Cited as the classic work by Benal Diaz del Castillo, which chronicles the invasion of Mexico by Cortez and his conquistadores in the 16th Century. Diaz reports that he witnessed a ceremony in which some of his Spanish compadres were sacrificed by Aztec priests, and then butchered; chunks of conquistadore meat were thrown to the populace, and these people rushed home and cooked them with hot peppers, wild tomatoes and a herb that apparently was oregano. That, my friends, is seriously set down as the true origin of chili. I dislike having to say it, but if you are going to adopt this recipe, it must begin, "First, catch yourself a lean Spaniard."

I know of only one Texan who has the facts straight on the origin of chili—Charles Ramsdell, author of an excellent history of San Antonio. It is clear from his delvings, as well as my own, that chili con carne had its happenings in San Antonio. Was it a dish contrived by Mexicans of old San Antonio de Bejar? No. Was it put together by white Texans? Not at all. You'd never guess in eight centuries. Chili was invented by Canary Islanders. In the 1720's the Spanish were in command of the town, which they had founded, but the French were pushing in from the East, and an appeal went out to the King of Spain to send some settlers. The king obliged halfheartedly, shipping sixteen families out from the Canary Islands. They established themselves in rude huts on the spot now known as the Main Plaza. In their homeland, these people were accustomed to food made pungent with spices. They liked hot peppers and lots of garlic, and they were acquainted with oregano. So they looked around to see what was available in foodstuffs in their new home, and they came up with a stew of beef and hot peppers and oregano and garlic and, I make bold to believe, tomatoes and onions and beans. It is my guess, too, that they managed to get hold of some cumin seed, which comes chiefly from North Africa. That's the way it happened, and any Texas historians who dispute me can go soak their heads.

There are friends incarnate, mostly Texans, who put chopped celery in their chili, and the Dallas journalist Frank X. Tolbert, who has been touted as the Glorious State's leading authority on chili, throws in corn meal. Heaven help us one and all! You might as well throw in some puffed rice, or a handful of shredded alfalfa, or a few maraschino cherries.

Let it be understood that I am well disposed toward Texans and enjoy visiting their state; I'm tolerant of all their idiotic posturing, of every one of their failings, save only this arrant claim of superiority in the composing of chili. Mr. Tolbert, of Dallas, who appears to be spokesman for a group called the International Chili Appreciation Society, declares that acceptable chili should contain no tomatoes, no onions and no beans. This is a thing that passeth all understanding, going full speed. It offends my sensibility and violates my mind. Mr. Tolbert criticizes Lyndon Johnson's chili recipe because it leaves out beef suet and includes tomatoes and onions. Yet the President's chili contains no beans. To create chili without beans, either added to the pot or served on the side, is to flout one of the basic laws of nature. I've been told that when I was a baby and it came time to wean me, I was fed Eagle Brand milk with navy beans frappéed into it. Thereafter, all through childhood and adolescence, I ate beans three or four times a week. If Chili Bill, back there in Illinois, had served his chili without beans, I would surely have deserted him and bought chocolate sodas for my lunch.

Texas has at least one chili scholar owning a glimmer of intelligence: Maury Maverick, Jr., son of the former Mayor of San Antonio and Rooseveltian Congressman. The younger Maury is a lawyer, and a true chili man in one respect—he speaks out against other chili cooks, saying, for example, of California chili: "With all that goddamn sweet stuff in it, it's like eating a strawberry sundae."

As for Southern California, my friend Fred Beck, a gourmet and semi-professional wine taster, adduces evidence to suggest that Los Angeles is the chili capital of the world. (The title, by the way, is claimed by San Antonio, and by the little town of Terlingua in the Big Bend country, and lately by Dallas.)

Mr. Beck tells me that chili was once called "size" in the town known to him as Lil-ole-ell-ay. "Size" came into usage by way of one Ptomaine Tommy, once proprietor of the largest and best-known chili parlor in the city. Ptomaine Tommy served straight chili and an epical Southwestern variation, a hamburger smothered with chili. He had two ladles, a large and a small. When a customer ordered straight chili, he got out the large ladle. When he wanted the other, he usually said, "Hamburger size." So Ptomaine Tommy put up one sign that said HAMBURGER SIZE 15¢, and another that said CHILI SIZE 20¢. Other chili joints followed suit, and before long chili was known throughout Los Angeles as "size." They'd say, "Just gimme a bowl of size."

Mr. Beck speaks, too, of the era when the architecture went kooky in Los Angeles, and commercial structures were designed to suggest the nature of the trade conducted within. There was a building on Pico shaped like a coffeepot, with steam issuing from its spout. A weenie stand on La Cienega was a large hideous representation of a frankfurter. Then came the chain of Chili Bowls. It was quickly noted by the always perceptive Angelenos that these structures were shaped like giant chamberpots, sans handles, so it became customary to say, "Let's drive over to the pot for a bowl of chili."

During my probings into the story of chili I stumbled on a fact that made my heart leap. There is a town called Chili in my state, New York. Texans pay not even lip service to their chili, for they have no town of that name. As for the New York community, just west of Rochester (there is also a North Chili nearby), I was soon disillusioned.

I telephoned my friend Judge Ray Fowler of Rochester, "Why did they call the town of Chili by that name?" I asked him.

"Never heard of it," he replied. "How do you spell it?"

I spelled it.

"Oh," he exclaimed, "you mean Chy-lye. The early settlers named it in honor of Chile's breaking away from Spanish rule."

"So," I said, "they misspelled it, and then mispronounced it. And it has nothing whatever to do with chy-lye con carne?"

"Nothing at all."

Just writing about this makes me disconsolate, so let us pass on to the chy-lye that comes in a bowl. The secret of making superior chili lies first in the ingredients and second in the genius of the cook. Nothing should ever be measured. Experimentation is the thing. Those blessed Canary Islanders in San Antonio wouldn't have known a measuring spoon from an electric carving knife. Spanish cookbooks never issue peremptory orders, for that would not be polite. They speak of "maybe fifteen centavos' worth" of parsley, a handful of so-and-so, and maybe a bunch of butter, and a few "teeth" of garlic if you have some in the house.

My daughter follows my haphazard methods and turns out chili that is the sensation of her set. She says she passes my recipe along to her chili-loving friends, and converts the ignorant to it, and all hands proclaim it to be the best of all possible chilis. That's what she tells me. Whenever I hear those heartwarming reports I feel so bucked up that I give her a trip to Mexico or Puerto Rico. Much the same thing happens in the case of my son, though he tells me he composes my chili with the doors locked and the shades drawn. He lives in Texas. For a time I wanted to establish that lovely tradition, the old family recipe, a secret that wild horses couldn't drag out of my descendants. A family is not a true entity unless it has in its archives a fabulous secret recipe. But my formula is out, and rapidly spreading, so I give it to the world.

Chili H. Allen Smith

Get three pounds of chuck, coarse ground. Brown it in an iron kettle. (If you don't have an iron kettle you are not civilized. Go out and get one.) Chop two or three medium-sized onions and one bell pepper and add to the browned meat. Crush or mince one or two cloves of garlic and throw into the pot, then add about half a teaspoon of oregano and a quarter teaspoon of cumin seed. (You can get cumin seed in the supermarket nowadays.) Now add two small cans tomato paste; if you prefer canned tomatoes or fresh tomatoes, put them through a colander. Add about a quart of water. Salt liberally and grind in some black pepper and, for a starter, two or three tablespoons of chili powder. (Some of us use chile pods, but chili powder is just as good.) Simmer for an hour and a half or longer, then add your beans. Pinto beans are best, but if they are not available canned kidney beans will do—two 15–17 oz. cans will be adequate. Simmer another half hour. Throughout the cooking, do some testing from time to time and, as the *Gourmet Cookbook* puts it, "correct seasoning." When you've got it right let it set for several hours. Later you may heat it up as much as you want, and put the remainder in the refrigerator. It will taste better the second day, still better the third, and absolutely superb the fourth. You can't even begin to imagine the delights in store for you one week later.

I deem it a pleasure to have given you my recipe for chili. I can only say in conclusion that some people are born to the tragic life. There are three distressing physiological mistakes made by nature: the vermiform appendix, the prostate gland, and the utter inability of many people to eat chili because of delicate digestive tracts.

I really bleed for them.

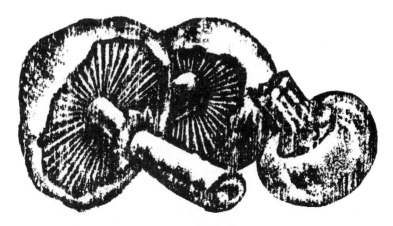

The Best of the Best
The Championship Recipes

Whether or not H. Allen Smith's challenging (to Texans, at least) article actually perpetrated the great chili wars is unclear; they may have sprung up without the story. But once they did get started, they spread like wildfire. There are now chili cookoffs in nearly every state of the Union and in such unlikely spots as Tahiti and New York's Fifth Avenue. They range from the deserts to the prairies to the swank Balboa Bay Club in Newport Beach, California. Then, when the states are through picking the best they have to offer, they all get together in the "big one," the World Championship Chili Cookoff.

One would think that chili can be made in only a limited number of ways—and for the most part that is accurate—but even championship chili seems to vary greatly from one section of the country to another. Just what it is that elevates one particular chili to the championship category still can't be determined. A poll of chili judges across the entire country failed to elicit a satisfactory explanation, so we have selected twenty-three championship recipes—as broad a cross section as possible—from state and national cookoffs so you can draw your own conclusions.

The recipes do not follow the standard format of the book because they are exactly the way the champions wanted them printed. They are hot and mild; they are simple and complicated (one, in particular, is so complex that it would take a true chili fanatic to even attempt it). But most of all, the recipes are winners. And they have that one ingredient that all winning recipes have. Perhaps it's not one that goes into the pot, but, rather, one that goes into the cook.

AUTHORS' NOTE: Substitutions of specific brand names may be made when that particular brand is not available.

Woodruff DeSilva's 1968 World Championship Chili

5 medium-sized onions, chopped
Small amount cooking oil
Salt and pepper to taste
4 pounds chuck beef, coarsely ground
5 cloves garlic, minced
4 tablespoons oregano
2 teaspoons woodruff (an herb)
1 teaspoon cayenne
2 tablespoons paprika
3 tablespoons cumin powder
Scant tablespoon to full tablespoon New Mexico brand chili powder
Scant to full teaspoon chipenos (known as chilipiquines), crushed

4 dashes Tabasco sauce
3 10-ounce cans tomato sauce
6-ounce can tomato paste
Water
4 tablespoons flour or masa flour

Brown onions with oil in a large skillet. Add salt and pepper. Transfer to a chili pot. Brown beef in a skillet. Add more oil if necessary. Add garlic and 1 tablespoon oregano. Transfer beef to pot. Combine woodruff, cayenne pepper, paprika, cumin, New Mexico chili powder, remaining 3 tablespoons oregano, and chipenos. Add the blended spices to the chili pot. Add Tabasco sauce, tomato sauce, and tomato paste. Add enough water to cover the meat, simmering at least 2 hours.

Reheat the chili to boiling. To thicken the mixture, add a little water to the flour to make a paste. Stir the paste into the mixture, stirring constantly to prevent sticking or scorching. Add water as necessary for the desired texture.
Serves: 6 to 8.

Wick Fowler's 1970 World Championship Chili

2 pounds meat, coarsely ground or diced
8-ounce can tomato sauce
2 cups water
1 package of 2-Alarm Chili Ingredients*
Salt

Sear the meat until it becomes gray. Add tomato sauce and water. Add all the ingredients except the masa flour. Cover kettle and simmer 1 hour and 15 minutes, until meat is tender. Stir occasionally. Skim off excess grease. Mix masa flour with warm water into a smooth paste. Stir into chili to "tighten" it and add flavor. Simmer 15 to 20 minutes and salt to taste. Chili is ready to serve.

For 1-Alarm, use only half of the red pepper. For False-Alarm Chili, leave out the red pepper. For 3-Alarm Chili or hotter, merely add hot pepper.
Serves: 6.

*2-Alarm Chili mix is available in many areas. It was developed by the late Wick Fowler, but for obvious reasons, the exact ingredients cannot be released by the Caliente Chili Company of Austin, Texas, who packages and distributes the mix.

Howard Winsor's 1972 World Championship Chili

1 medium-sized onion, chopped in blender
5 or 6 large cloves garlic, chopped in blender
½ cup water
2 pounds lean beef, cut into ¼-inch cubes
1 pound pork, cut into ¼-inch cubes
7-ounce can Ortega brand green chiles, including liquid
5 or 6 jalapeño peppers
1 can, No. 2, tomatoes, whole, chopped in blender (14½ oz.)
1 can, No. 303, tomatoes, whole, chopped in blender (16 oz.)
4 large bay leaves
1 tablespoon oregano
1 tablespoon salt
1 teaspoon cumin powder

Chop onion, garlic, and water in a blender. Cook until soft. Add meat; cook until it loses red color. Add green chiles and jalapeño peppers to the blender and puree to make a chili pulp. Add 1 cup chili pulp and tomatoes to meat; cook 20 minutes. Add other seasonings. Remove bay leaves about halfway through cooking time. Use covered pot; you might have to remove lid last part of cooking time if too thin. Total cooking time, approximately 3 hours. If you want to use beans, put in bottom of bowl before adding chili.
Serves: 6 to 8.

Joe DeFrates's 1973 and 1975 World Championship Recipe

1 pound ground beef
1 1¼-ounce envelope of Chilli Man Chilli Mix*
8-ounce can tomato sauce
1 dash Tabasco sauce

Brown ground beef in heavy skillet. Stir in contents of chili mix and add tomato sauce. Simmer for 1 hour and add Tabasco.

*Joe DeFrates originally developed the Chilli Man Mix (the Illinois spelling of *chili*) and sold it, packaged, under that name from the 1950s until he sold the recipe to the Milnot Company of Litchfield, Illinois, in the 1970s. It is available today in most midwestern states under the original name. Again, the actual ingredients of the chili mix are not available.
Serves: 4.

Allegani Jani Schofield McCullough's 1974 World Championship Chili

4 pounds stew meat, ground once
3 onions, chopped
2 tablespoons oil
Salt and pepper to taste
2 heaping teaspoons cumin seed
6 cloves garlic, mashed
12-oz. can tomatoes
1 teaspoon sugar
½ can beer
2 packs Vanco brand chili seasoning
1 small pack Vanco brand chili powder
3 teaspoons molé paste (available in stores stocking Mexican foods)
1 teaspoon Tabasco sauce
1 teaspoon salt
1 quart water
4 jalapeño peppers, chopped
½ cup masa flour

Brown meat and onions in oil. Season with salt and pepper. Using a *molcajete* (a Mexican grinding tool), grind cumin seed and garlic with a little water. Add to meat. Combine tomatoes, sugar, beer, chili seasoning, chili powder, and molé paste and blend in a blender. Add to stew. Add Tabasco, salt, water, and jalapeño peppers. Cook 2½ hours, stirring often. Combine masa paste with a little water to a runny paste. Add paste to stew to thicken, stirring quickly to prevent lumps. Cook 30 minutes longer.
Serves: 8.

Rudy Valdez's 1976 World Championship Chili

1 pound pork shoulder, chopped into ⅜-inch pieces
1 pound beef flank steak, chopped finely but not ground
1 teaspoon cumin powder, divided into 2 portions
1 ripe tomato, chopped
1 clove garlic, minced
1 medium-sized white onion, chopped
6 stalks celery, 6 inches long, chopped
8-ounce can Ortega brand green chile salsa
8-ounce can Ortega brand green chile peppers, diced
1 teaspoon oregano
1 teaspoon Tabasco sauce
1 tablespoon hot New Mexico brand chili powder
1 tablespoon medium New Mexico brand chili powder
1 heaping tablespoon mild New Mexico brand chili powder
Water
Salt to taste

Cook pork and beef in separate pans for 20 minutes. Add ½ teaspoon cumin to each skillet. Combine tomato, garlic, onion, celery, chile salsa, green chiles, oregano, and Tabasco sauce in a 6-quart saucepan. Make a paste, adding a small amount of water, with the three grades of chili powder. Combine to the vegetable mixture, blending well. Cook 20 minutes. Drain juice from skillet, except 4 tablespoons. Add meat to vegetable mixture. Cook 1½ hours until meat is tender. Prior to serving, add salt to taste.
Serves: 6.

Jay Pennington's 1977 World Championship Chili

1 tablespoon cooking oil
3 medium-sized onions, minced
2 green peppers, minced
2 stalks celery, minced
3 cloves garlic, minced
8 pounds round steak, coarsely ground
2 No. 2 cans tomato sauce (14½ oz.)
2 No. 2 cans stewed tomatoes (14½ oz.)
2 No. 2 cans water (14½ oz.)
6-ounce can tomato paste
4-ounce can chile salsa
1 3-inch green canned hot pepper, minced (only 1 chile
  from the can)
2 3-ounce bottles chili powder
4-ounce can diced green chile
Dash of oregano
Salt to taste (approximately 3 tablespoons)
Pepper to taste (coarse ground)
Garlic to taste

Heat oil in a 10- to 12-quart pot. Add onion, green pepper, celery, and garlic. Cook until onion is transparent. Add meat gradually, stirring until redness disappears. Add remaining ingredients, stirring after each addition. Lower heat, simmer 2½ to 3 hours, stirring frequently to prevent scorching.
Serves: 12 to 16.

"Nevada Annie" Harris's 1978 World Championship Chili

3 medium-sized onions
2 medium-sized green peppers
2 large stalks celery
2 small cloves garlic
½, or more, small fresh jalapeño pepper
8 pounds lean chuck, coarsely ground
7-ounce can diced green chiles
2 14½-ounce cans stewed tomatoes
15-ounce can tomato sauce
6-ounce can tomato paste
2 3-ounce bottles chili powder
2 tablespoons cumin powder
Tabasco sauce to taste
12-ounce can beer
12-ounce bottle mineral water
2 to 3 bay leaves
Garlic salt
Salt and pepper to taste

Dice and sauté first five ingredients. Add meat and brown. Add remaining ingredients, including ½ can beer (drink the remainder, says Annie). Add water just to cover top. Cook about 3 hours on low heat. Stir often. Freezes well.
Serves: 12 to 16.

Joe and Shirley Stewart's 1979 World Championship Chili

3 pounds round steak, coarsely ground
3 pounds chuck steak, coarsely ground
1 cup vegetable oil or kidney suet
Pepper to taste
3-ounce bottle chili powder
6 tablespoons cumin powder
1 teaspoon MSG
6 small cloves garlic, minced
2 medium-sized onions, chopped
Water
6 dried chile pods. Remove stems and seeds, boil 30
   minutes in water. (Or 3-ounce New Mexico brand
   chile pepper)
1 tablespoon oregano brewed in ½ cup beer (like
   tea)
2 tablespoons paprika
2 tablespoons cider vinegar
3 cups beef broth
4-ounce can Ortega brand green chiles
½ can, 14-½-ounce, stewed tomatoes (or to taste)
1 teaspoon Tabasco sauce (or to taste)
2 tablespoons masa flour

Brown meat in oil or suet adding pepper to taste. Drain
meat. Add chili powder, cumin, MSG, garlic, and onion.
Cook 30 to 45 minutes using as little water as possible.
Add water only as necessary. Stir often. Remove skins
from boiled pods, mash pulp, and add to meat mixture.
Add strained oregano-beer mixture, paprika, vinegar, 2
cups beef broth, Ortega green chiles, stewed tomatoes,

and Tabasco sauce. Simmer 45 minutes, stirring often. Dissolve masa flour into remaining beef broth, pour into chili. Simmer 30 minutes, stirring often.
Serves: 10 to 12.

Denver Whisman's West Virginia Championship Chili

> 1 pound ground pork
> 1½ pounds ground chuck
> 5 teaspoons salt
> 1 tablespoon black pepper
> 3 pounds beef stew chunks
> 4 red onions, chopped
> 7 green peppers, chopped
> 2 28-ounce cans whole tomatoes
> 1 2¼-ounce jar chili powder
> 2-ounce bottle Tabasco sauce
> 1 teaspoon crushed pepper
> 6 ounces pure honey

Brown pork, chuck, salt, and black pepper in a 3-gallon pot. Mix with a potato masher. Add beef chunks, stirring intermittently. Cook 10 minutes. Add red onions, cook covered, 25 minutes. Add green peppers, cook 10 minutes. Add tomatoes, cook 20 minutes. Stir in chili powder, Tabasco sauce, and crushed pepper, cook 30 minutes covered. Stir occasionally for 1 hour, uncovered. Add honey 15 minutes before serving.
Serves: 4 to 6.

Carolyn Blakemore's Championship Hillbilly Chili

1½ pounds ground beef
1½ pounds ground chuck
1 onion, chopped
1 green pepper, chopped
1 stalk celery, chopped
16-ounce can stewed tomatoes
8-ounce can A&P brand Spanish tomato sauce
8-ounce can tomato sauce
1 can College Inn beef broth (14½ oz.)
1 or 2 cans (depending on taste) Old El Paso brand
    tomato and green chiles
2 tablespoons oregano
3 tablespoons chili powder
1 tablespoon cumin powder
¼ cup sugar
¼ teaspoon salt
¼ teaspoon pepper
1 teaspoon celery salt
1 teaspoon onion salt
3 cups water

Brown meat with onion, pepper, and celery in a heavy skillet. Drain off fat. Mix spices with stewed tomatoes, tomato sauces, beef broth, and water in a 6-quart Dutch oven. Add browned meat and cook until thick.
Serves: 6.

Dr. Randy Jouno's Guadalajara, Mexico, Championship Chili
ALSO GOLDEN CHILE PEPPER AWARD WINNER

¼ cup oil
4 pounds top round steak, trimmed into ¼-inch cubes
6 cups water
5 6-ounce cans tomato paste
½ cup instant minced onion
2½ tablespoons celery salt
3 tablespoons chili powder
½ teaspoon ground allspice
½ teaspoon ground cinnamon
½ teaspoon curry powder
½ teaspoon garlic powder
½ teaspoon coriander seed, ground
½ teaspoon cumin seed, ground
½ teaspoon ground ginger
½ teaspoon marjoram leaves, crushed
½ teaspoon oregano leaves, crushed
½ teaspoon paprika
½ teaspoon thyme leaves, crushed
½ teaspoon sage leaves, crushed
Pinch red pepper, ground
27-ounce can whole green chiles, drained, seeded, and chopped
4-ounce bar milk chocolate, broken up

Heat 2 tablespoons oil in a large saucepan until hot. Add 1 pound beef and brown on all sides. Remove with a slotted spoon and set aside. Repeat until all beef is browned. Use additional oil as needed. Return all beef to saucepan. Add 4 cups water, tomato paste, onions, celery salt, spices, herbs, and green chiles; mix well. Boil, then

reduce heat and simmer, covered, for 90 minutes, stirring occasionally. Add remaining water. Mix in chocolate; simmer, covered for 30 minutes, stirring often.
Serves: 6.

Tony Palermo's Michigan Championship Chili

5 pounds ground beef
3 tablespoons oil
6 cloves garlic, crushed
3 large onions, chopped
3 green peppers, chopped
6 jalapeño peppers, chopped
¾ cup chili powder
¼ cup oregano
¼ cup sweet basil
¼ cup thyme
¼ cup crushed rosemary
1 tablespoon salt
1 tablespoon white pepper
1 tablespoon cumin powder
2 No. 10 cans (gallon each) whole tomatoes (13 lbs.)
1 cup tomato paste
1 teaspoon Tabasco sauce
Sour cream for garnish

Brown ground beef, drain, and set aside. Heat oil and sauté garlic, 2 chopped onions, green peppers, and jalapeño peppers. Cook on medium heat for 5 minutes. Add all spices. Continue cooking for about 3 minutes. Add whole tomatoes and juice, tomato paste, Tabasco, and beef and cook for 2½ hours. Garnish with sour cream and chopped onions.
Serves: 12.

Max Vallejo's Oregon Championship Chili

2 tablespoons salad oil
1 pound filet mignon, cut into ⅜-inch cubes
1 pound flank steak, cut into ⅜-inch cubes
1 pound ground top sirloin, cut into ⅜-inch cubes
2 15-ounce cans tomato sauce
1 chorizo (Spanish sausage)
¹⁄₁₆ teaspoon ground red pepper
1 medium-sized red onion, chopped
1 medium-sized white onion, chopped
6 scallions or green onions, chopped
2 medium-sized tomatoes, chopped
1 stalk celery, finely chopped
2 garlic cloves, minced
2 teaspoons chili powder
½ teaspoon onion powder
½ teaspoon garlic powder
½ teaspoon tarragon leaves, crushed
½ teaspoon celery seed
½ teaspoon thyme leaves, crushed
½ teaspoon cumin seed
½ teaspoon cumin powder
½ teaspoon parsley flakes
½ teaspoon salt
¼ teaspoon savory leaves, crushed
¼ teaspoon herb seasoning, crushed
¼ teaspoon curry powder
¼ teaspoon oregano leaves, crushed
¼ teaspoon turmeric
⅛ teaspoon paprika
⅛ teaspoon ground black pepper
2 whole cloves
½ bay leaf

In a large skillet, heat oil. Add filet; brown quickly on all sides (meat should be red on the inside); remove with slotted spoon, set aside. Add flank steak; brown quickly on all sides; remove with a slotted spoon; set aside. Add sirloin to skillet; cook and stir until brown; remove with a slotted spoon; set aside. In a heavy cast-iron saucepot, heat tomato sauce until hot. Remove sausage from casing; chop. Add to tomato sauce along with reserved filet; simmer for 1 minute. Add flank steak; cover and simmer for 3 minutes. Add sirloin; cover and simmer for 20 minutes. Add red and white onions, scallions, tomatoes, celery, and garlic. Cover and simmer for 20 minutes. Add seasonings; cover and simmer for 15 minutes. Remove cover and simmer for 15 minutes longer.

Serves: 4 to 6.

Joe Burgoz's Colorado Championship Chili

INDIAN CHILI

5 pounds beef, chopped into small cubes
3 pounds pork, chopped into small cubes
6 tablespoons lard
5 cloves garlic, chopped
2 large onions, chopped
2 medium-sized bell peppers, chopped
2 yellow chiles
4 long green chiles
2 tablespoons flour
4 tablespoons red chili sauce
1 8-ounce can hot tomato sauce
2 tablespoons prepared mustard
2 tablespoons vinegar
2 tablespoons Worcestershire sauce
1 tablespoon cumin powder
Dash of oregano
2 medium cans beef broth
2 tablespoons salt
1 tablespoon pepper

Brown meat in 2 tablespoons lard in a large skillet. Pour into chili pot. In another 2 tablespoons lard, sauté garlic, onions, bell peppers, and chiles. Add to chili pot. Heat remaining 2 tablespoons lard in skillet. Add flour and brown. Pour in chili sauce. Stir until smooth; pour into chili pot. Bring to boil; add other ingredients. Cook slowly 2½ hours, stirring often.
Serves: 12 to 16.

Hy Abernathy's Georgia Championship Chili

6 pounds lean beef, coarsely ground
3 cups tomato sauce
1 quart burgundy wine
4½ teaspoons chili powder
½ large onion, minced
4 large mushrooms, finely chopped
2 tablespoons cooking oil
4 teaspoons garlic powder
1 teaspoon oregano
Dash cumin powder
Dash rosemary
1 to 4 teaspoons MSG
½ to 2 teaspoons cayenne
½ teaspoon black pepper
¼ cup masa or flour
Salt to taste

Sear meat to golden brown in large skillet. Transfer meat to 1½-gallon kettle. Add tomato sauce and 2 cups burgundy wine and heat to boiling. Sauté onions and mushrooms with oil in a skillet. Mix in garlic powder and pour into meat mixture. Mix in all remaining spices, except pepper and salt. Add 1 cup burgundy and cook for 30 to 40 minutes, stirring constantly. Make a thin paste of flour and water and add to mixture, stirring every 5 minutes. Mix in remaining 1 cup burgundy and continue stirring. Add tap water as necessary to thin mixture. Add pepper and salt to taste during last hour. Cook on low heat 3 to 6 hours.
Serves: 10 to 12.

Carl Moore's Arizona Championship Chili

ROAD RUNNER CHILI

1 teaspoon vegetable oil
3 large yellow onions, chopped
1 pound pork, coarsely ground
½ ounce cumin powder
6 pounds beef sirloin, coarsely ground
46-ounce can tomato juice
1 package Carroll Shelby Texas brand Chili Preparation*
¼ teaspoon oregano
4 ounces Durkee's chili powder
½ ounce paprika
4 cloves garlic, minced
½ ounce garlic powder
1 can beer
¼ teaspoon dry mustard
1 ounce celery flakes
4 canned jalapeño peppers

Put about a teaspoon of oil in a large saucepot. Sauté onions. Add the pork to the onions and stir to brown. Add a little of the cumin. Add beef; brown, adding a little more cumin. Add tomato juice, stirring to blend, then add all remaining ingredients. Allow mixture to cook over low heat for 2 or 3 hours.
Serves: 10 to 12.

*Carroll Shelby's Texas Chili Preparation is available in most markets in the West.

Bill Gasper's Illinois and Missouri Championship Chili

1 large onion, finely chopped
2 large celery ribs, finely chopped
2 small carrots, finely chopped
2 cloves garlic, minced
2 tablespoons Ortega brand jalapeño peppers, finely
   chopped
½ cup oil
3 pounds ground chuck
2 pounds beef chuck, cut into ½-inch cubes
5 tablespoons chili powder
1 teaspoon oregano
1 teaspoon garlic powder
¼ teaspoon rosemary, ground
¼ to ½ teaspoon Tabasco sauce
¼ can beer
2 8-ounce cans tomato sauce
½ to 1 cup water
Salt and pepper to taste

Combine onions, celery, carrots, garlic, and jalapeño peppers in a large skillet with the oil and sauté until tender. Remove vegetables from oil and set aside. Brown beef, small amounts at a time, until all meat is browned. Place beef and vegetables into a large pot and add remaining ingredients. Cover and simmer, stirring often, for several hours. Season to taste.
Serves: 6 to 8.

Angee Scaramuzzo's Lower Colorado Championship Chili

CHILI SCARAMOUCHE

2 coots from Lake Havasu*
1 can beer
2 large onions, chopped
3 cloves garlic, minced
3 ounces Crisco
3 pounds pork roast, deboned and ground
7 pork chops, lean and cut into ½-inch cubes
3 pounds ground chuck roast
1 green pepper, chopped
1 stalk celery, chopped fine
4 ounces green chiles, diced
4 ounces jalapeño relish
4 ounces *napalitos en escabeche***
12-ounce can whole tomatoes, chopped
36-ounce can tomato juice
4 tablespoons cumin powder
1 tablespoon oregano
1 tablespoon cayenne
2 tablespoons Anaheim brand chili powder
2 tablespoons New Mexico brand chili powder
4 tablespoons monosodium glutamate
Salt and pepper to taste

Boil coots in seasoned water and beer. In large pot, sauté onions and garlic in Crisco until they are tender. Add meat and brown. Add coot broth and remaining ingredients. Cook slowly for 3 hours. Makes six quarts.
Serves: 12.

* and ** The champion says coots from any other place simply won't do, but if you want to risk the chance

and you don't have the time to travel to Lake Havasu, well . . . Also, she informs us that *napalitos en escabeche* is pulp from a 3,000-year-old cactus from the foothills of the Mohave Mountains in Topock, Arizona. The decisions are yours.

Ham Flannagan's Virginia Championship Chili

3 tablespoons butter
2 to 3 jalapeño peppers, chopped
2 to 4 garlic cloves, crushed
2 to 3 large onions, sliced
3 to 4 pounds diced sirloin or fillet steak
Pinch oregano
Olive or peanut oil
1½ to 2 ounces chili powder
28-ounce can tomatoes
3½ to 4½ cups water, added as needed
Cayenne to taste
3 secret ingredients (a dollop of sherry wine, blackstrap molasses, cornmeal mash made into a paste with water)
Salt and pepper to taste
Cumin powder
Worcestershire sauce

Sauté peppers, garlic, and onion in butter. Add Worcestershire and cumin to taste. In Dutch oven or large skillet, brown meat chunks along with oregano and chili powder. Add first mixture (onions, etc.), tomatoes, chili, and water as needed. Bring to a boil rapidly, while stirring constantly. Reduce heat to very low while stirring, and add secret ingredients to taste. Add corn paste or arrowroot to thicken if desired. Stir constantly and taste often.
Serves 6.

Bob Ozaki's Hawaiian Championship Chili

½ cup oil
4 pounds beef roast, cut into ⅜-inch cubes
3 pounds pork butt, cut into ¾-inch cubes
2 pounds Portuguese sausage, cut into ½-inch cubes
4 cloves garlic, finely chopped
2 ribs celery, chopped
2 green peppers, cut into ⅜-inch pieces
3 medium-sized onions, chopped
16 ounces beer
1 tablespoon ground oregano
2 tablespoons cumin powder
¼ teaspoon MSG
2 tablespoons black pepper
2 tablespoons Hawaiian salt (rock salt)
10 tablespoons chili powder
1 teaspoon thyme
1 teaspoon minced cilantro (Chinese) parsley
1 teaspoon minced green onions
4 10-ounce cans chicken broth
2 14½-ounce cans stewed tomatoes
2 8-ounce cans tomato sauce
2 6-ounce cans tomato paste
2 4-ounce cans diced green chiles
1 tablespoon chili powder
2 bay leaves
1 teaspoon kiawe (Hawaiian) honey
1 pound Cheddar cheese, grated
Juice of 1 lime
½ cup finely chopped green onions
½ small Maui (sweet, mild) onion, finely chopped

Heat oil in a large skillet and brown small amounts of beef cubes. Remove browned pieces to a large pot. Repeat

until all beef is browned. Repeat for pork and sausage until all are browned and added to pot. Reserve oil in skillet. Sauté garlic, celery, green pepper, and onions in oil until tender. Transfer vegetables to pot. Combine beer with seasonings and let stand 2 minutes. Add seasonings and beer to beef mixture. Add remaining ingredients to pot and simmer for 3 hours, stirring every 15 minutes. Add ¾ pound grated Cheddar cheese to chili and stir. Save remaining cheese for garnish. Add the juice of 1 lime and stir. Combine ½ cup green onions and ½ small Maui onion in a small bowl. To garnish chili, sprinkle with onions and grated Cheddar cheese.
Serves: 8 to 10.

Tahiti Championship Chili

3 large onions, minced
1 clove garlic, run through a press
4-ounce can diced green chiles
2 pounds hamburger
2 tablespoons cumin seeds
Dash red pepper
16-ounce can tomatoes (plus juice)
3 8-ounce cans tomato sauce
4-ounce can tomato paste
1¾ ounces mild chili powder
Dash of ground cloves
Water
½ teaspoon MSG
2 tablespoons hot chili powder

Combine onions, garlic, and green chiles and set aside. Brown beef in a large skillet and add onion mixture.

Simmer 30 minutes. Add cumin seed and red pepper. Stir well. Add tomatoes, tomato sauce, and paste. Stir well. Add chili powder, cloves, and enough water to thin to desired thickness. Add MSG and simmer about 35 minutes. Cover and simmer 2 hours, stirring often. Before serving add hot chili powder and stir again.
Serves: 4 to 6.

Floyd Cunningham's "German Red" Oklahoma Championship Chili

6 pounds beef, coarsely ground
1 cup chili powder
2 tablespoons ground oregano
2 tablespoons ground *comino* (cumin)
2 tablespoons salt
1 tablespoon coriander
2 tablespoons garlic powder
2 quarts water
½ cup yellow cornmeal
4 capsules vitamin E supplement, 100 I.U. each*
1 pound Floyd's German Smoked Sausage, cubed
    (see p. 59)

Cook meat until it turns gray, then add all spices and stir. Add water and heat to a boil. Reduce heat and let simmer for 2 hours. Stir in cornmeal; if too thick, add water to suit. Add Floyd's German Smoked Sausage and heat for 30 minutes. (Hot country sausage may be substituted for Floyd's, if necessary.)
Serves: 10 to 12.

*Floyd says it gives his chili a message.

Floyd's German Smoked Sausage

10 pounds pork shoulder, fresh
2 pounds beef arm roast
½ cup brown sugar
1 tablespoon black pepper
½ bottle Wright's brand liquid smoke
1 teaspoon red pepper
1 tablespoon garlic powder
½ cup Morton's Sugar Cure (smoke flavor)

Cut meat in 1-inch cubes. Mix all spices in meat; let set in refrigerator overnight. Grind through coarse grinder plate, then make a sausage patty and fry for sample taste; at this time, add more spices if necessary. When spices are correct, grind a second time through fine plate. Stuff into pork casings (available at selected meat markets), and place in refrigerator overnight. Smoke with hickory wood at 250° for 1 hour.*

*Oklahoma chili champion Floyd Cunningham says, "I smoke mine in a large Char-Broil cooker. Start charcoal, then place wood over charcoal until wood starts to burn, then put lid down and adjust vents so smoke will go over sausage."

What's Hot and What's Not— How to Select and Prepare the Ingredients

There seems to be exactly as many chili recipes as there are chili cooks; but one thing that most agree on is that the two most important ingredients in any chili are the chile peppers and the chili powder—the *e* and the *i* of chili.

As in any form of cooking, selecting and preparing *fresh* ingredients gives the dish an edge over one featuring canned or frozen ingredients. In the case of chili, however, it is not always possible to find the fresh ingredients; unless, of course, you live in New Mexico or California, and then it is seasonal. So, for some, at least, canned or frozen will have to do—and will probably do nicely.

If you are fortunate enough to live in an area where they are grown, buy fresh peppers; and you can even make your own blend of chili powder. Here is what is normally available (fresh, canned, or frozen), how to select and prepare them, and how to store them:

Fresh Chile

Green: The first fresh green chile peppers of the season bring premium prices. In the Southwest—particularly New Mexico—mature, high quality chile is ready to market in mid to late July. Fresh green chile remains on the counters of markets and roadside stands until frost.

Red: The season for fresh red chile peppers is naturally shorter than for green chile. Some producers market their entire crop as fresh ripe chile, and many market part of their crop green and the remainder red. Keeping in mind that the chile first goes through the green stage, the season for red chile is usually from September until frost.

Frozen Chile (and related items)

Sauces: Green and red chile sauces are available in most frozen foods cabinets of local markets. Labels of some are more informative than others about ingredients.

Combination dishes: Along with chile, these often contain beef or cheese in combination with tortillas or spaghetti. Green and red enchiladas are popular combination dishes.

TV dinners: Sometimes labeled "Mexican Dinners," the number of these full-meal frozen items is great. The labels list the foods included.

Chile: Frozen chopped or whole chiles, ready-to-use, are available in some markets.

Specialty items: These include such foods as cocktail tacos and burritos.

Canned Chile

Whole pods: Some companies label the packs as mild or hot but do not indicate the variety. These are packed in 4-ounce, 10-ounce, and No. 2½ cans. Two or three pods usually fill a 4-ounce can.

Chopped: This product is excellent when the recipe calls for chopped chile. The label may note the pungency of the chile. Four- and 10-ounce cans are common.

Sauces: Not all canners list the ingredients of their canned sauce, nor do they always indicate their pungency. Red and green chile sauces are available, usually in 4-ounce and 10-ounce cans.

Dry Red Chile

This is a staple item in markets throughout the country. The dried red pods may be sold whole or ground into powder. The materials used for packaging dried red chile are variable as are the weights of the packs. The weight, however, is noted on the package. Labels of some packs indicate the pungency of the chile, although the labels are not consistently informative. Shoppers almost always need to know whether chile is mild or hot, regardless of its form—fresh, frozen, canned, or dried. By telling their retailers or writing to processors, shoppers can indicate that they want to select chile according to its pungency. Certified seed of the various varieties are available to producers. From this beginning, chile can be correctly labeled as to its pungency as it moves through the channels of trade.

Selecting Chiles

Fresh: Large, smooth pods with well-rounded smooth shoulders are easy to peel and there is little waste in them. Firm, mature, and thick-fleshed pods with a bright shiny surface have good texture, flavor, and vitamin content. Avoid immature, shriveled, dull-appearing, or ill-shaped pods, as they are usually diffi-cult to peel, may lack characteristic flavor, and may be lower in vitamin content.

Dried, whole pods: High-quality dry chile is an even red color. Select pods free of black mold spots to avoid waste.

Dried, powder: High-quality ground chile is an even red color. Yellow indicates that seeds are included.

Storing the Chiles

For best flavor, texture, vitamin value, and ap-pearance, buy fresh chile, green or red, in amounts that will be used within three days. Freshly gathered pods peel more easily than those kept for a few days. Crisp pods peel more easily than wilted, limp ones. Store chile in polyethylene-type bags in the refrigerator until time to prepare.

Store frozen chile products at zero temperature or lower. Protect purchases of frozen items from thawing from market to home freezer. Texture, flavor, ap-pearance, and nutrient content of chile are lowered when it is allowed to thaw and refreeze.

Store canned chile in a cool, dark place before it is opened; refrigerate after opening, and use it within a day or so to avoid loss of flavor and vitamin content.

Store dried red chile or chili powder in a cool, dark place. Dried red chile, like any other spice or herb, loses flavor and appearance when stored at warm room tem-peratures.

Canning and Freezing

Fresh green and red chile cans and freezes well. Such products are valuable sources of vitamin A and C. Vitamin C is lost in dried red chile.

Some prefer to blister and peel chiles before packing for freezing and canning. The practice of blistering the pods and then packing and freezing them unpeeled is growing, however. The chile is peeled later, when it is used. Freezing the blistered, unpeeled pods reduces the preparation time for freezing. Also, fewer pods are broken. Apparently the thin skin, although blistered, serves as a shield and results in attractive pods for such use as *chiles rellenos*. Though no research is available on the possible development of off-flavors, it is suggested that any pods with charred skins be removed from packs of unpeeled chiles.

Chiles, like all other low-acid vegetables, must be pressure-canned to be safe.

Peeling Chiles

There is no single way to remove the tough, transparent outer skin from chiles. A few accepted practices, however, make an easy job of the process:

First, put on rubber gloves.

Slit one side of each chile pod. To lower the pungency, remove seeds and veins before the pods are blistered.

Put chiles on a cookie sheet or a pan and place under the broiler 3 to 5 inches below the broiler element. Use high position of electric range or medium flame of gas range. Leave oven door open. Turn pods frequently for even blistering. Do not burn chiles.

Or you can blister the pods this way: Place heavy wire mesh on surface burner of range. Use high position of electric range or medium flame of gas range. Place chiles on wire mesh, turning frequently for even blistering.

Or: Blister chiles on the outdoor grill following a family cookout, again turning frequently, so as not to burn them.

For crisp green chile, remove blistered pods from pan or grill and plunge into ice water. For more thoroughly cooked chiles, place them in a pan and cover with a damp towel to steam for 10 to 15 minutes.

Starting at stem end, peel outer skin downward.

Chili Powder

Chili powder is simply chile pepper with other spices added. For the most part, the average chili powder comprises 80 percent chile pepper, along with garlic powder, ground oregano, ground cumin seed, and a little salt. Some more exotic blends incorporate pinches of clove, allspice, anise, and coriander.

Truly serious chili cooks blend their own chili powder, creating as distinctive a blend as the very ingredients in their own chili.

By using the above ingredients, in one combination or percentage or another, you can develop your own personal chili powder. It may be a trial-and-error process, but the end result will be your own unique chili powder. Or, by the same process of elimination, you can select your favorite already prepared chili powder from the several available on grocery shelves; either way, your chili powder should be just that: *your* chili powder, not merely the first one you come to.

Chili–From a Bowl of Red to the River Thames

The forty-seven just-plain-good chili recipes in this section graphically demonstrate the phenomenal versatility of chili as it is prepared around the world. The dish, as the vast array of recipes indicates, can include anything from the traditional meat and spices and tomatoes to any combination of ingredients, some prosaic, some exotic (honey, zucchini, rattlesnake, armadillo, tequila, and bourbon, to name a few). There are simple recipes and ones that require a foray into the Epicurean shops; there are mild varieties and recipes that only the heartiest leather-tongues dare taste.

Many of the names herald the recipe's heritage. Others are simply euphonic—from Chili Caliente California to Abilene Chili. And you can bet that if a chili is named Buzzard's Breath, it is hot.

Whatever kind of chili one desires can be found in these pages: a simple bowl of Texas Red or chili from the frozen Northland of Minnesota; a mild blend, a hot one, a midnight snack chili, or a breakfast chili; a way to perk up canned chili, diet chili, or microwave chili. It is, after all, America's favorite dish.

AUTHORS' NOTE: There is no structure whatsoever to cooking or even planning good chili. The only "law" of chili is the total absence of any law at all. If there are basic ingredients at all, they have to be meat (almost any kind), chili powder, onion, garlic, and chiles (canned or dried). The basic chili recipe in chapter one (page 7) is a good one to consider as a starter; but we predict that you will be improvising before you get to the stove. Chili is that way.

Chili with White Beans

A mild, slightly sweet chili.

3 pounds ground beef
6 cups water
1 bay leaf
6 cloves garlic, minced
2 teaspoons salt
1 teaspoon oregano
½ teaspoon cayenne
2 tablespoons paprika
1 teaspoon cumin powder
½ pound dry navy beans
1 teaspoon brown sugar
1 tablespoon chili powder

Brown beef thoroughly. Add all the remaining ingredients and cook over low flame for 4 hours. Add more water if mixture becomes too thick.
Serves: 6.

Texas Red

If there were but one name for chili, it would be "Texas Red."

3 pounds round steak, cut into ¼-inch cubes
¼ pound suet
1 tablespoon Mexican oregano
3-ounce bottle chili powder
1 tablespoon cayenne
1 tablespoon cumin seed, crushed
1 clove garlic, minced
1 tablespoon Tabasco sauce
6 medium-sized tomatoes, chopped
6 jalapeño peppers, chopped
2 quarts water
4 tablespoons masa flour (dilute with 2 tablespoons water to make a paste)

In heavy pot, brown together steak and suet, until redness is gone from meat. Add oregano, chili powder, cayenne, cumin seed, garlic, and Tabasco; mix well. Add tomatoes, jalapeños, and enough water for desired consistency. Simmer, uncovered, for 2 hours, stirring frequently. Skim off fat; add masa flour paste and simmer for 45 minutes, adding more water if necessary.
Serves: 6.

Ranch House Chili

Adapted from an original Wyoming ranch house recipe;
slightly more complicated than the cattle trail blend.

1 pound dry pinto beans
3 pounds fatty ground beef
1 large green pepper, chopped
1 large onion, chopped
2 cloves garlic, crushed
3 pounds fresh tomatoes, peeled
1 tablespoon cumin seed
¼ teaspoon Tabasco sauce
4 tablespoons chili powder
2 cups water

Rinse pinto beans and place in a shallow saucepan. Cover with water and allow to soak overnight. The next day brown meat with green pepper, onion, and garlic in a large Dutch oven. Add tomatoes, cover, and cook for 30 minutes. Add pinto beans, cumin seed, Tabasco, chili powder, and water. Blend well. Cook 2 hours uncovered at low heat.
Serves: 6.

Chili Colorado

Mashing the beans hides them from the purist.

> 2 pounds fillet, steak cut into ¼-inch cubes
> 3 tablespoons corn oil
> 1 medium-sized onion, minced
> 4 cloves garlic, minced
> 2 teaspoons salt
> 2 tablespoons cumin powder
> 5 tablespoons chili powder
> 2 tablespoons masa flour
> 2 teaspoons brown sugar
> 1 16-ounce can kidney beans, mashed
> 16-ounce can tomatoes, undrained and squeezed
> 6-ounce can tomato paste

Sauté fillet cubes in corn oil. Remove from skillet and set aside. Add onion, garlic, salt, cumin, chili powder, and masa flour to oil and blend until smooth. Add brown sugar, kidney beans, tomatoes, and tomato paste, stirring until all ingredients are well blended. Add meat and stir again. Cover, stirring frequently, for 1 hour. *Serves: 4.*

Santa Fe Chili

From an original cattle trail recipe.

¼ **pound suet, ground**
6 pounds beef, cut into ½-inch cubes
4 ounces chili powder
3 tablespoons cumin powder
2 tablespoons salt
1 tablespoon cayenne
⅓ **cup finely ground cornmeal**
1 tablespoon oregano
3 cloves garlic, minced
1 cup beef broth
2 cups sour cream

Render suet for drippings, discard casing. Add beef and chili powder to drippings and brown. Add cumin, salt, cayenne, and cornmeal, blending well. Reduce heat to low. Add oregano, garlic, and beef broth. Stir until thickened. Serve with fresh sour cream on the side.
Serves: 8 to 10.

Buzzard's Breath

An old chili term for very hot blends.

> ¼ pound suet (no casing), ground
> 4 pounds flank steak, cut into ½-inch cubes
> 3 large onions, chopped
> 3 cloves garlic, chopped
> 1 quart water
> 8 whole tomatoes, chopped
> 6-ounce can tomato paste
> 8 California chili pods, chopped
> 2 tablespoons crushed red pepper seeds
> ½ cup chili powder
> Salt to taste
> 2 tablespoons masa flour

Render suet in large skillet and add steak cubes and cook over medium heat until cubes are brown. To large pot, add steak and all remaining ingredients except masa flour; stir to mix well. Bring to a boil and reduce heat; simmer, uncovered, for 2 hours, stirring often. Make paste of masa flour and stir into chili. Simmer, uncovered, for another 15 minutes.
Serves: 8.

Missouri Mule-Skinner Chili

An old Joplin recipe, using white beans.

> 1 pound dry white beans
> ½ pound sausage, ground
> ½ pound bacon, cut into ¼-inch pieces
> 1 medium-sized onion, minced
> 3 cloves garlic, minced
> 3 quarts water
> 1 tablespoon salt
> 2 tablespoons chili powder
> 16-ounce can tomatoes, chopped
> 4-ounce can green chiles, chopped
> 1 teaspoon cumin powder
> 1 teaspoon coriander

Fry white beans with sausage and bacon until all meat is browned. Add onion and garlic. Cook until onion is tender. Add water, salt, chili powder, tomatoes, green chiles, and spices. Stir well. Cover and simmer for 2 hours, stirring frequently.
Serves: 4.

General Alarm Chili

One for the die-hard leather-throats.

⅓ pound suet, chopped
3 pounds beef, cut into 1-inch chunks
2 large onions, chopped
1 clove garlic, minced
1 quart water
16-ounce can whole tomatoes, chopped
8-ounce can tomato sauce
6-ounce can tomato paste
6 tablespoons chili powder
8 jalapeño peppers, chopped
7-ounce can diced green chiles
2 tablespoons Tabasco sauce
1 teaspoon cayenne
½ cup vinegar
¼ cup cornmeal

In large skillet, render suet and discard casing; add beef chunks, onion, and garlic and cook over medium flame until beef has lost its redness. Transfer beef mixture to a large kettle. Add remaining ingredients; stir to mix well. Bring to a boil and reduce heat. Simmer, covered, for 1½ hours, stirring frequently. Skim off enough fat to satisfy taste.
Serves: 6 to 8.

Louisiana Filé Chili

The subtle filé taste is reminiscent of Creole cookery.

½ cup beef fat
3 pounds round steak, cut into ¼-inch cubes
3 cloves garlic, minced
1½ onions, chopped
3 jalapeño peppers, chopped
1 green pepper, minced
2 green tomatoes, peeled and cubed
½ cup chopped mushrooms
⅓ cup coriander
6 teaspoons cumin powder
⅓ teaspoon filé
¼ teaspoon cayenne
2 teaspoons salt
3 cans beef stock
12-ounce can tomato paste
¼ cup cornmeal

Render fat for drippings, discard fat casing. Brown beef cubes in fat drippings. Add garlic, onions, jalapeño peppers, and green peppers to beef. Sauté until onions are tender. Add tomatoes, mushrooms, coriander, cumin, filé, cayenne, and salt to mixture. Combine beef stock, tomato paste, and cornmeal in a separate bowl, blending well. Add beef stock to meat mixture; stir until well blended. On low heat cook 2 hours, uncovered, stirring frequently.
Serves: 6.

Cactus Chili

The tequila adds the needles.

> ½ cup flour
> 4 teaspoons salt
> ¼ teaspoon pepper
> 3 pounds pork shoulder, cut into 1-inch cubes
> ¼ cup oil
> ¼ cup instant minced onions
> ¼ teaspoon instant minced garlic
> 1 cup water
> 16-ounce can tomatoes, chopped
> 4 ounces tequila
> 1½ tablespoons chili powder
> 1 teaspoon cumin seed, ground (optional)
> 2 16-ounce cans kidney beans, drained
> ½ cup golden raisins

Combine flour, 2 teaspoons salt, and pepper in a large bowl. Add pork and toss, coating each piece thoroughly. Shake off excess flour and reserve. Heat oil in a heavy skillet. Brown thoroughly one third of the meat at a time. Combine dried vegetables with water to rehydrate. Add vegetables to pork drippings and brown. Add tomatoes, tequila, and stir well. Add chili powder, cumin, and reserved flour to tomatoes, blending well. Bring to a boil. Reduce heat, cover, and simmer 1 hour. Add beans and raisins, simmer 10 minutes. Serve over steamed rice garnished with sliced avocado and shredded Cheddar cheese, if desired.
Serves: 6 to 8.

Rio Grande Chili

A hot Texas variety.

2 pounds ground round
1½ teaspoons salt
2 tablespoons oil
3 tablespoons cumin seed
1 tablespoon paprika
2 tablespoons Tabasco sauce
2 cloves garlic, minced
2 onions, chopped
3 tablespoons masa flour
2 7-ounce cans diced green chiles
3 tablespoons chili powder
12-ounce can beer
10-ounce can beef broth

In a large skillet, brown ground round and salt in heated oil. Add cumin seed, paprika, Tabasco, garlic, and onions to beef. Sprinkle mixture with masa flour. Toss gently. Add green chiles and chili powder. Add beer and broth. Mix well to blend all ingredients. Add water if mixture is too thick. Cook covered for 2 hours, stirring occasionally.
Serves: 4 to 6.

Franklin County White Lightning Chili

. . . from the hills of Virginia.

> 2 pounds lean ground chuck
> 1 pound ground pork, cut into ½-inch cubes
> 1 pound lean lamb, cut into ½-inch cubes
> 1 cup moonshine
> 2 cups ginger ale
> 2 teaspoons Tabasco sauce
> 1 teaspoon marjoram
> 1 teaspoon cayenne
> 1 tablespoon garlic powder
> Salt to taste
> 1 tablespoon dry mustard
> 2 ounces chili powder
> 3 cups minced onions
> 1 cup minced celery
> 1 cup minced green peppers

Combine meats in pot and add moonshine, ginger ale, Tabasco, marjoram, cayenne, garlic powder, salt, mustard, and chili powder. Mix well. Let stand for 1 hour, then simmer for 30 minutes. Combine onions, celery, and green pepper and add to meat. Cook, covered, for 1 hour over low heat. Stir thoroughly and cook, uncovered, over low heat for 1 more hour.
Serves: 6 to 8.

Dante's Inferno Armadillo Chili

One of the hot ones.

¼ cup salad oil
2 pounds beef stew meat (chuck or round), cut into
  1-inch cubes
1 pound armadillo meat (preferably nine-banded armadillo), cut into 1-inch cubes
3 large onions, chopped
3 cloves garlic, minced
1 quart water
8-ounce can tomato sauce
6-ounce can tomato paste
½ cup chili powder
8 jalapeño peppers, chopped
4 chile pods, dried
1 tablespoon Tabasco sauce

Heat oil in large saucepan or kettle. Add beef, armadillo,
onion, and garlic; cook until meat is browned. Add
remaining ingredients; stir to mix well. Bring to a boil
and reduce heat. Simmer, uncovered, for 2 hours or until
meat is tender. Stir occasionally.
Serves: 8.

Tex-Mex Chili

Tex-Mex is rapidly becoming a popular school of cooking, combining the best of two cultures.

> 3 tablespoons oil
> 1½ pounds stew beef, cut into ¼-inch cubes
> 1 green pepper, seeded and cubed
> 1 medium-sized onion, chopped
> 16-ounce can beef broth
> 2 7-ounce cans Ortega brand green chile salsa
> 3 tablespoons chili powder
> ½ teaspoon cumin powder

Brown beef with oil in a large skillet. Add vegetables and cook until tender. Add beef broth, chili powder, and cumin. Cover and cook at medium heat for 2 hours. Remove cover, simmer longer for desired thickness, stirring often.
Serves: 4.

Sheepherder's Chili

Adapted from an old Montana recipe.

> 2 pounds ground lamb
> 1 cup chopped onions
> ¾ cup chopped green peppers
> 2 medium cloves garlic, minced
> 28-ounce can tomatoes, chopped
> 1 tablespoon salt
> 1 bay leaf
> 1 tablespoon chili powder
> 2 4-ounce cans Ortega brand diced green chiles
> 16-ounce can pinto beans, drained

Brown lamb in a large skillet until crumbled. Drain. Add onion, green pepper, and garlic, and cook until vegetables are tender. Stir in remaining ingredients except beans. Simmer, covered, for 35 minutes, stirring occasionally. Remove cover and add beans. Simmer, uncovered, 10 minutes, or until desired consistency. Garnish with sour cream or Monterey Jack cheese, if desired.
Serves: 6 to 8.

Philadelphia Chili

The salt pork flavor lingers.

> ¼ pound salt pork, cut into thin strips
> 2 pounds ground chuck
> 2 medium-sized green peppers, chopped
> 1 medium-sized onion, chopped
> 2 16-ounce cans whole tomatoes, chopped
> 16-ounce can kidney beans
> 4 tablespoons chili powder
> 6-ounce can tomato paste
> 1 teaspoon Tabasco sauce
> 1 quart water
> Salt and pepper to taste

Cook salt pork and ground chuck together in skillet until ground meat is browned. Set aside. In large pot, sauté green peppers and onions, using small amount of salt pork grease; stir in tomatoes and kidney beans. Add chili powder, tomato paste, Tabasco, and enough water to create desired consistency. Stir in meat (including salt pork strips) and simmer, uncovered, for 2 hours, stirring frequently. Salt and pepper to taste.
Serves: 6.

Buffalo Chili

A modern "Old West" recipe.

2 pounds buffalo, cut into ½-inch cubes
2 medium-sized onions, chopped
1 green pepper, seeded and minced
1 tablespoon celery salt
1 tablespoon garlic salt
1 tablespoon salt
3 tablespoons A–1 sauce
4 tablespoons apple cider vinegar
1 tablespoon Worcestershire sauce
2 tablespoons brown sugar
2 teaspoons chili powder
1 teaspoon pepper
1 teaspoon red pepper
½ teaspoon paprika
1 teaspoon oregano
16-ounce can tomato sauce
12-ounce can tomato paste
Water

Brown meat, onion, and green pepper in a large skillet; cook until vegetables are tender. Add remaining ingredients, cover, and simmer for 20 minutes. Stir occasionally. Add 3 to 4 cups water for desired consistency, cover, simmer for 3 hours or until it suits your fancy.
Serves: 4 to 6.

AUTHORS' NOTE: Beefalo or cattalo may be substituted for buffalo.

Hot Rod Chili

From the editors of Hot Rod *magazine.*

1½ pounds lean beef
½ pound lean pork
1 large onion
1 large clove garlic
1 large bell pepper
2 tablespoons bacon grease or oil
8-ounce can tomato sauce
16 ounces beer
6 to 8 tablespoons red chili powder
1 tablespoon paprika
2 tablespoons cumin powder
2 tablespoons oregano
1 tablespoon salt
4 ounces diced green chiles
1 teaspoon cayenne or ground dry red pepper
⅓ cup masa flour

Grind the beef and pork, using coarse blade of chopper, or cut into small pieces and pound with meat mallet. Chop the onion and green pepper, and run the garlic through a garlic press. Put all these ingredients into a Dutch oven or heavy deep pot with the grease or oil. Cook until meat is brown. Add the tomato sauce and the beer. Simmer for 30 minutes. Add remaining ingredients except the masa flour. Simmer 1 hour, stirring occasionally. If more liquid is needed, add beer as desired. Mix masa flour with a little beer to make thin paste and stir this mixture into the chili.
Serves: 4 to 6.

Chocolate Chili

May have been why the phrase "Don't knock it until you've tried it" was coined.

2 pounds ground chuck
2 pounds ground pork
2 large green peppers, chopped
1 large onion, chopped
1 clove garlic, minced
¼ cup bacon drippings
8 medium-sized tomatoes, chopped
½ teaspoon Tabasco sauce
4 tablespoons chili powder
2 cups water
2 1-ounce squares Mexican chocolate (or sweet chocolate with a pinch of cinnamon and ginger), grated

To large pot, add ground chuck, pork, green peppers, onion, and garlic and cook over medium heat in bacon drippings for 10 minutes. Add tomatoes, Tabasco, chili powder, and water and simmer, uncovered, for 2 hours. Stir in chocolate and serve.
Serves: 8.

Goober Pea Chili

Originated in Alabama, not Georgia, where peanuts are called Goober peas.

> 3 pounds fatty ground beef
> ¼ pound suet (no casing), ground
> 1 large green pepper, chopped
> 2 large onions, chopped
> 1 clove garlic, minced
> 2 16-ounce cans whole tomatoes, chopped
> 4 red hot Italian peppers, chopped
> 4 tablespoons chili powder
> 2 cups water
> 1 cup small Redskin type peanuts

Brown beef in suet and reserve in skillet. In saucepan, add green pepper, onions, garlic, tomatoes, red peppers, and chili powder and cook over medium heat, stirring often, for 15 minutes. Add meat and enough water for desired consistency and simmer, covered, for 1½ hours, stirring frequently. Add peanuts and cook, uncovered, over low heat for 15 minutes.
Serves: 6.

Outback (Australian) Chili

This recipe is supposed to have been developed by a couple of Australian tennis players while in California, but is now popular Down Under.

3 pounds kangaroo meat, cut into ¼-inch cubes
¼ cup coconut oil
1 cup chopped onion
3 cloves garlic, minced
4 tablespoons cumin seed
1 teaspoon salt
2 teaspoons paprika
1 cup bamboo shoots
½ teaspoon white pepper
2 pounds cherry tomatoes, quartered
2 10½-ounce cans beef bouillon
1 teaspoon dry mustard

In a very large pot, brown meat in oil until golden brown. Add remaining ingredients and stir thoroughly. Bring quickly to a boil; reduce flame and slowly cook for 2 hours or until meat breaks apart easily.
Serves: 6.

NOTE: Pork may be substituted if kangaroo meat is unavailable—but then you have to change the name of the dish!

Eye-Opener Chili

True chili lovers can eat it 'round the clock, so here's an easy breakfast chili.

2 tablespoons butter
1 medium-sized onion, chopped
1 teaspoon garlic salt
¼ teaspoon salt
½ teaspoon oregano leaves, crushed
4 large tomatoes, peeled and chopped
¼ teaspoon Tabasco sauce
2 tablespoons chili powder
16-ounce can kidney beans and liquid
6 eggs
6 corn muffins, split and toasted

In skillet, melt butter. Add onion and garlic and cook until tender. Add ¼ teaspoon salt, oregano, tomatoes, Tabasco, chili powder, and kidney beans and simmer 30 minutes. Break eggs, one at a time, into a cup, being careful not to break yolks, and ease into simmering sauce. Cover and simmer 10 minutes or until eggs are poached. Carefully spoon one egg and ample sauce over each muffin.
Serves: 6.

Microwave Chili

It had to happen . . .

1 pound ground beef
1 cup chopped onions
½ cup chopped green peppers
1 clove garlic, minced
¾ teaspoon salt
16-ounce can whole tomatoes, drained and chopped
16-ounce can kidney beans, undrained
¼ cup seeded, green chile peppers, chopped
2 tablespoons tomato paste
2 tablespoons chili powder
½ teaspoon cumin powder

Crumble ground beef into a 2-quart glass or microwave-proof casserole. Add onion, green pepper, garlic, and salt; mix well. Cover and cook about 8 minutes, stirring several times. Stir in tomatoes, beans, chiles, tomato paste, chili powder, and cumin. Cover. Cook 8 to 10 minutes, stirring twice during cooking. Let stand, covered, 3 minutes before serving.
Serves: 4.

Diamondback Chili

Oddly—or alarmingly—rattlesnake is found in many chili recipes.

2½ pounds roast beef, cut into 1-inch cubes
2 cups rattlesnake meat, cut into ¼-inch cubes
½ cup masa flour
¼ cup cornmeal
1 teaspoon salt
1 teaspoon pepper
4-ounce jar chili powder
2 cups beef suet, ground
3 onions, chopped
4 cloves garlic, crushed
2 tablespoons cumin powder
1 teaspoon oregano
4 15½-ounce cans beef broth

Combine meats and let stand at room temperature for 2 hours. Combine masa flour, cornmeal, salt, pepper, and chili powder, blending well. Dredge meat in flour mixture. Render suet at high heat. Drop several pieces of meat into hot fat, browning well. Continue until all meat is browned. Remove all meat from skillet and add onions and garlic to drippings. Sauté at low heat until vegetables are tender. Return meat to skillet and add beef broth. Add remaining flour to mixture, stir to blend. Simmer 2½ to 3 hours. Stir frequently.
Serves: 6 to 8.

50,000-Watt Chili

. . . if you like the malty taste of beer.

4 pounds beef shoulder, cut into 2-inch cubes
3 cans beer
10 dried chiles, chopped
1 large onion, chopped
3 cloves garlic, minced
3 jalapeño peppers, chopped
16-ounce can tomato paste
1 teaspoon salt
3 tablespoons barbecue sauce
1½ teaspoons oregano
2 teaspoons cumin powder
Water

Place beef in a pressure cooker. Add beer. After steam starts to escape, reduce flame to low and cook 2 hours. Remove meat and shred. Add chiles, onion, garlic, and jalapeño peppers to pot. Return lid and cook under pressure 20 minutes. Remove lid and add remaining ingredients. Cook uncovered 1 hour. If mixture is too thick add ½ to 1 cup water or to desired consistency. *Serves: 6 to 8.*

Sausalito Chili

The rice and artichoke hearts make this one interesting.

⅓ cup instant minced onions
¼ cup sweet pepper flakes
½ cup water
1 tablespoon oil
1 pound lean ground beef
7 teaspoons chili powder
1 teaspoon salt
½ teaspoon ground black pepper
⅛ teaspoon garlic powder
24-ounce can tomatoes, chopped
8 marinated artichoke hearts
½ teaspoon oregano leaves
½ teaspoon sugar
2 cups hot cooked rice

Cover instant onion and sweet pepper flakes with water for 10 minutes to rehydrate. Heat oil in a large skillet and sauté vegetables 3 minutes. Add meat, chili powder, salt, black pepper, and garlic powder. Stir and cook 5 minutes or until meat loses red color. Add tomatoes and simmer 5 minutes. Stir in artichoke hearts, oregano leaves, and sugar. Cook 10 to 15 minutes. Serve over hot cooked rice.
Serves: 4 to 6.

Abilene Chili

A complex recipe with a hearty taste.

> **5 pounds stew beef**
> **3 onions, minced**
> **⅓ cup olive oil**
> **1 tablespoon salt**
> **2 teaspoons seasoning salt**
> **1 teaspoon pepper**
> **6 cloves garlic, minced**
> **1 teaspoon sugar**
> **16-ounce can tomatoes**
> **1 can beer**
> **3 tablespoons hot chili powder**
> **3 tablespoons cumin powder**
> **5 tablespoons paprika**
> **1 tablespoon Tabasco sauce**
> **1 tablespoon oregano**
> **¾ cup masa flour**
> **6-ounce can tomato paste**
> **½ teaspoon celery seed**
> **3 jalapeño peppers, chopped**
> **1 bay leaf**
> **3 tablespoons cornmeal**
> **1 teaspoon coriander seed, ground**
> **3 quarts beef broth**
> **2 tablespoons cayenne**

Brown meat and onions with olive oil in a large Dutch oven. Add salts, pepper, garlic, and sugar. Cover and simmer for 2 hours. Remove meat and cube. Return meat to Dutch oven. Add tomatoes, beer, chili powder, cumin, Tabasco, and oregano. Stir well. Combine masa flour with tomato paste, blend well. Add 1 cup drippings from the pot to the tomato mixture, blending until smooth. Add tomato mixture to the pot and blend well. Add celery seed, jalapeño peppers, bay leaf, cornmeal, and coriander to the pot. Slowly add beef broth. Cook uncovered at medium heat until thickened. Reduce heat, cover, and cook for 3 hours, stirring often. Add cayenne just before serving.

Serves: 8 to 10.

Boston Chili (with Beans)

A very mild blend, featuring eggplant.

1½ **pounds ground beef**
4 **cups water**
2 **16-ounce cans kidney beans**
28-ounce can tomatoes, undrained
6-ounce can tomato paste
1 **small eggplant, peeled and cut into** ½-inch **cubes**
½ **green pepper, chopped**
1 **large onion, minced**
2 **tablespoons chili powder**
1 **teaspoon salt**
½ **teaspoon pepper**

Brown meat in a large skillet. Crumble into small pieces. Add remaining ingredients, simmer 2 hours, stirring occasionally.

Serves: 4.

Hoosier Hot

This comes directly from Gasoline Alley, but, because of the intense spiciness, is probably of Southwest heritage.

> ¼ cup cooking oil
> 2 pounds stew beef
> 2 pounds ground pork
> 3 large onions, chopped
> 2 cloves garlic, minced
> 3 cups water
> 2 16-ounce cans whole tomatoes, chopped
> 6-ounce can tomato paste
> 3-ounce bottle chili pepper
> 6 chili pods, dried
> 2 tablespoons Tabasco sauce
> 1 teaspoon cayenne
> 6 red Italian peppers

In large skillet, heat oil. Add beef and pork, onions, and garlic and cook until meat is brown, stirring often. Add meat and remaining ingredients to large kettle; stir to mix well. Bring to a boil and reduce heat. Simmer, uncovered, for 1½ hours, stirring occasionally.
Serves: 8.

El Paso Chili

A milder blend that doesn't lose its zesty flavor.

3 pounds ground beef
7 ounces beer
2 teaspoons salt
2 teaspoons pepper
2 teaspoons paprika
½ teaspoon sage
2 teaspoons sugar
1 tablespoon cumin powder
4 tablespoons chili powder
3 tablespoons A–1 sauce
½ cup vinegar
1 tablespoon soy sauce
2 16-ounce cans tomatoes, chopped
12-ounce can tomato paste
⅓ cup cornmeal
1½ pounds pork shoulder, cubed
1 tablespoon garlic powder
7-ounce can Ortega brand diced green chiles
2 jalapeño peppers, diced

Brown beef thoroughly. Add beer, salt, pepper, paprika, sage, sugar, cumin, and chili powder, blending well. Cover and simmer 2 hours. Add remaining ingredients, cover, and simmer over low flame for 3 hours, stirring frequently.
Serves: 6 to 8.

Chili Oriental

. . . combines two diverse cultures.

> 2 pounds pork shoulder, cubed (do not trim fat)
> ½ pound round steak, cubed
> 2 large green peppers, chopped
> 2 large onions, chopped
> 2 stalks celery, diced
> 4 cups beef broth
> 1 8-ounce can bamboo shoots
> 1 8-ounce can water chestnuts, sliced
> 1 teaspoon pepper
> 2 tablespoons chili powder
> 4 ounces soy sauce
> 3 tablespoons cornstarch
> 1 small package bean sprouts
> 8 mushrooms, sliced

Brown pork with pork fat in a large skillet. Add beef and brown with peppers, onions, and celery. Cover and simmer 20 minutes, until onions are transparent. Stir frequently. Add beef broth, bamboo shoots, water chestnuts, pepper, and chili powder. Blend. Combine soy sauce with cornstarch until smooth. Pour slowly into meat mixture while stirring. Continue stirring until thickened. Add remaining ingredients. Cover, stirring frequently, and simmer 2 hours or until meat is tender. *Serves: 4 to 6.*

Italian Chili

1½ pounds ground beef
½ pound pepperoni, ground
½ pound Italian sausage, ground
2 cups chopped onions
1 tablespoon minced garlic
1 large eggplant, peeled and cubed
1 cup zucchini, chopped
15-ounce can tomato sauce
8-ounce can whole tomatoes, chopped
2 teaspoons oregano
3 tablespoons chili powder
¼ teaspoon thyme
Salt and pepper to taste
½ cup freshly chopped parsley
½ cup Parmesan cheese
½ cup Marsala wine

Brown beef, pepperoni, and Italian sausage in a large skillet. Break meat into small pieces and stir often. Transfer meat to a large pot and cook at low heat. Reserve drippings in skillet. Add onion, garlic, eggplant, and zucchini to drippings. Sauté until onions are tender. Transfer eggplant mixture to pot with meat mixture. Add drippings also. Add tomato sauce, tomatoes, oregano, chili powder, thyme, salt and pepper. Simmer for 2 hours, stirring occasionally. Add parsley, Parmesan cheese, and Marsala wine. Cook at medium heat for 30 minutes.
Serves 6 to 8.

Savannah Chili

The bacon adds an unusual flavor.

6 strips bacon
1 pound dry pinto beans
2 quarts water
5 pounds lean ground beef
1 cup chopped onions
2 medium-sized green peppers, chopped
3-ounce bottle chili powder
2 teaspoons cumin powder
1 teaspoon marjoram
1 teaspoon oregano
1 teaspoon red hot pepper
1 teaspoon salt
1 teaspoon pepper
4 shakes Tabasco sauce
1 cup yellow cornmeal
1 pound fresh mushrooms, sliced
2 16-ounce cans tomatoes
6-ounce can tomato paste
4 cups water

Fry bacon crisp. Wash beans and cover with 2 quarts water. Crumble bacon and add, with drippings, to beans and allow to soak overnight. Brown beef in a large skillet, a little at a time, with green peppers, chili powder, cumin, marjoram, oregano, hot pepper, salt, pepper, and Tabasco. Transfer meat mixture to a Dutch oven and add cornmeal, mushrooms, tomatoes, tomato paste, and 4 cups water. Cover and simmer 3 hours, stirring often.
Serves: 8 to 10.

Kentucky Chili

The bourbon flavor fits in surprisingly well.

5 pounds beef chuck, cubed
½ cup oil
2 14½-ounce cans beef broth
6 ounces bourbon
2 cans beer
2 6-ounce cans tomato paste
2 large onions, chopped
8 large cloves garlic, minced
6 teaspoons cumin powder
2 teaspoons oregano
2 teaspoons salt
5 teaspoons coriander
10 tablespoons chili powder
2 teaspoons pepper
1 teaspoon sugar
2 bay leaves, whole
2 7-ounce cans Ortega brand diced green chiles
12 tablespoons masa flour

Brown meat, a handful at a time, with oil in a large skillet. Transfer browned meat to Dutch oven at low heat. Add bourbon, beer, and tomato paste, cover and simmer 20 minutes. Add onions and remaining ingredients except masa flour. Stir, cover, and simmer 2 hours, stirring often. Combine 2 cups chili liquid and masa flour, blending to a smooth paste. Slowly pour the paste into meat mixture to thicken. Add water if mixture is too thick to suit your taste.
Serves: 8 to 10.

Quick-and-Easy Chili

The simplest and tastiest way to pep up canned chili.

> 2 16-ounce cans chili without beans
> 7-ounce can Ortega brand diced green chiles
> 8 ounces grated Monteray Jack cheese

Combine canned chili and diced green chiles in a saucepan. Cook over medium heat, stirring occasionally, until hot and bubbly. Serve topped with cheese.
Serves: 4.

Diet Chili

Also a perfect after-the-game chili.

> 3 pounds lean ground beef
> 2 medium-sized onions, chopped
> 1 tablespoon vegetable oil
> 2 7-ounce cans diced green chiles
> ½ teaspoon garlic salt
> 3 tablespoons chili powder
> 6 whole tomatoes, chopped
> Water

In kettle, brown beef and onions in vegetable oil. Add chiles, garlic salt, chili powder, tomatoes, and enough water for desired thickness. Simmer 1 hour.
Serves: 6 to 8.

Macaroni Chili

Called "Chili Mac" in its native Ohio.

2 large onions, chopped
⅓ cup beef suet
2 pounds ground beef
½ cup macaroni
2 cups beef broth
16-ounce can tomatoes, chopped
16-ounce can kidney beans
¼ teaspoon garlic powder
½ teaspoon pepper
1 teaspoon paprika
2 tablespoons chili powder
1 teaspoon salt

Brown onion with suet in a large skillet. Add ground beef and cook until meat crumbles. Add macaroni, beef broth, and tomatoes. Stir well. Add beans, garlic powder, pepper, paprika, chili powder, and salt. Cover, simmer at low heat for 3 hours, stirring often. Serve with hot corn bread and a salad.
Serves: 4 to 6.

Chili Caliente California

The cabrito *adds a sweet flavor.*

3 tablespoons beef fat
2 cups chopped onions
8-ounce can hot chile peppers, minced
1 clove garlic, minced
2 pounds *cabrito* (goat), cut into ¼-inch cubes
4 cups chopped tomatoes
1 tablespoon sugar
2 teaspoons salt
¼ cup water
3 tablespoons chili powder
2 tablespoons A–1 sauce
16-ounce can kidney beans (plus juice)
2 stalks celery, minced

Heat fat in a large skillet. Add onions, hot chile peppers, garlic, and goat. Brown until onions are tender. Add remaining ingredients, cover, simmer for 2 to 3 hours (depending on desired thickness), stirring occasionally. Add water if mixture is thicker than you desire.
Serves: 4 to 6.

Zucchini Chili with Taco Chips

An unusual recipe featuring zucchini and corn.

1 medium-sized zucchini, chopped
¼ cup oil
2 pounds ground chuck
1 medium-sized onion, chopped
½ cup green pepper, chopped
2 teaspoons apple cider vinegar

1 teaspoon sugar
8-ounce can corn, whole kernel
16-ounce can pinto beans
¼ cup chili powder
6-ounce can tomato paste

Sauté zucchini in oil until transparent; remove and set aside. Brown beef, onion, green pepper, and vinegar in the zucchini drippings. Return zucchini to skillet, stir in remaining ingredients, and blend well. Cook on low flame for 2 full hours. Add liquid for desired thickness. *Serves: 4.*

Vegetable Chili

For the few who secretly prefer vegetable soup to chili.

3 pounds ground beef
1 cup chopped onions
2 green peppers, chopped
2 stalks celery, chopped
2 cloves garlic, minced
10-ounce tomato juice
16-ounce can tomatoes, chopped
16-ounce can kidney beans
½ teaspoon parsley
¼ teaspoon saffron
¼ teaspoon rosemary
1 teaspoon salt
¼ teaspoon pepper
1 tablespoon Tabasco sauce

Sauté beef, onion, peppers, celery, and garlic together until onions and peppers are tender. Cover and simmer for 1 hour. Add remaining ingredients and cook another 3 hours. Add water until desired consistency is reached. *Serves: 6.*

Baked Chili

Moves chili to the casserole category.

Chili:

> 3 tablespoons suet
> 2 pounds ground beef
> ⅓ cup green pepper, cut in strips
> 1 cup chopped onion
> 1 tablespoon chili powder
> 1 teaspoon salt
> ½ teaspoon pepper
> ½ teaspoon monosodium glutamate
> 1 bay leaf
> 1 clove garlic, chopped
> 16-ounce can kidney beans
> 2 cups tomatoes, chopped

Topping:

> ⅓ cup flour
> 2 teaspoons sugar
> ½ teaspoon baking powder
> ¾ cup yellow cornmeal
> 1 egg, beaten
> ⅓ cup buttermilk

Melt suet in a large, heavy pot. Add meat, peppers, onions, chili powder, salt, pepper, monosodium glutamate, bay leaf, and garlic. Brown meat mixture until peppers and onions are tender. Add beans, cover, and simmer for 1 hour. Stir occasionally.

Preheat oven to 375° F.

Combine flour, sugar, baking powder, and cornmeal until well blended. In a separate bowl, combine egg and buttermilk. Pour egg mixture into flour mixture and beat until smooth. Let stand for 5 minutes.

Pour chili filling into 9-by-13-inch cake pan. Spoon topping over chili and spread to touch sides. Bake for 30 minutes or until cornmeal crust turns golden.
Serves: 4 to 6.

Connecticut Chili

. . . shows the nationwide popularity of chili.

1 pound ground beef
½ pound ground pork
½ pound lean beef, cut into ¼-inch cubes
¼ cup oil
1 onion, chopped
1 green pepper, chopped
1 stalk celery, chopped
1 clove garlic, minced
2 8-ounce cans tomato sauce
2 cups water
4 tablespoons chili powder
2 teaspoons salt
2 teaspoons cumin powder
2 teaspoons Worcestershire sauce
2 tablespoons oregano
2 15-ounce cans kidney beans (plus juice)

Brown meats with oil in a large skillet. Add onion, green pepper, celery, and garlic. Cook onion-pepper mixture with meat until vegetables are tender. Add remaining ingredients, cover, and simmer for 2 hours, stirring occasionally.
Serves: 4 to 6.

Chili Fiesta

A mild blend for a large group. Place Tabasco sauce and cut-up jalapeño peppers on the table for those who prefer it hotter.

6 pounds ground beef
3 cups chopped onions
2 cups chopped green peppers
6 cloves garlic, minced
2 28-ounce cans tomatoes, chopped
8-ounce can tomato sauce
3 tablespoons salt
2 bay leaves
3 tablespoons chili powder
4 7-ounce cans Ortega brand diced green chiles
3 16-ounce cans pinto beans, drained
2 envelopes instant beef broth

Brown beef in an 8-quart saucepan until crumbled. Drain. Stir in remaining ingredients. Simmer, uncovered, 1 hour, or until desired consistency has been achieved. Garnish with sour cream or Monterey Jack cheese, if desired.
Serves: 10 to 12.

Cincinnati Chili

One of the most famous of all chili recipes.

1 quart beef broth
2 pounds ground beef
¼ cup onion flakes
4 tablespoons chili powder
1 teaspoon ground cinnamon
1 teaspoon ground cumin
¾ teaspoon instant minced onions
½ teaspoon salt
¼ teaspoon ground allspice
¼ teaspoon ground cloves
¹⁄₁₆ teaspoon ground red pepper
1 bay leaf
15-ounce can tomato sauce
2 tablespoons cider or white vinegar
½ ounce (½ square) unsweetened chocolate

Boil beef broth in a 4-quart saucepan. Slowly add beef to broth until meat separates into small pieces. Cover and simmer 30 minutes. Add onion flakes, chili powder, cinnamon, cumin, minced onions, garlic, salt, allspice, cloves, red pepper, bay leaf, tomato sauce, vinegar, and chocolate and mix well. Bring to a boil. Reduce heat, simmer, covered, 1 hour, stirring occasionally. Refrigerate overnight. Skim off fat before heating and serving. *Serves: 6.*

Minnesota-Style Chili

About as far North-of-the-Border as we found organized chili cooking.

1 clove garlic, mashed
1 teaspoon salt
1 cup chopped onions
2 tablespoons cooking oil
1 pound ground beef
1 tablespoon flour
⅛ teaspoon pepper
2 tablespoons chili powder
1 teaspoon oregano
15-ounce can kidney beans, drained
6-ounce can tomato paste
8-ounce can tomato sauce
1 cup water

Combine garlic with salt. Sauté onion in oil for 5 minutes. Add garlic, salt, and ground beef. Cook 10 minutes, stirring frequently. Add remaining ingredients. Simmer over low heat, stirring occasionally, 1 hour.
Serves: 4.

Chili Corpus Christi

A mild coastal *Texas recipe.*

> 1½ **pounds beef (fatty), cut into ½-inch cubes**
> 1½ **pounds pork, cut into ½-inch cubes**
> ¼ **cup olive oil**
> 3 **cups water**
> 1 **tablespoon paprika**
> 1 **tablespoon chili powder**
> 1 **tablespoon salt**
> 1 **tablespoon cumin powder**
> 1 **teaspoon brown sugar**
> 3 **cloves garlic, minced**
> 2 **cups beef broth**
> ⅓ **cup masa flour**
> ¼ **cup cornmeal**

Brown meats together in olive oil in a large skillet. Drain half the drippings. Place the meat in a medium-sized pot and add water and remaining ingredients. Cook for 2 hours over low heat, stirring occasionally. *Serves: 4 to 6.*

River Thames Chili

A British entry one year in the chili cookoff.

2 tablespoons vegetable oil
1 medium-sized onion, chopped
1 clove garlic, chopped
1 pound ground steak
2 teaspoons salt
1 teaspoon paprika
½ cup chutney
4 tablespoons *comino* (cumin), North African blend
8 large tomatoes, chopped neatly
2 pints consommé
1 teaspoon sugar
1 tablespoon Worcestershire sauce

Heat oil in large skillet; add onions and garlic and slowly cook until a warm brown color prevails. Add ground steak and uniformly sprinkle with salt and paprika. Cook until meat is brown, thoroughly smashing chunks with the back of a long fork. Add chutney, *comino,* tomatoes, consommé, sugar, and Worcestershire sauce and simmer, covered, for 45 minutes, stirring frequently. Serve with an ample supply of Wattney's Ale.
Serves: 4.

Celebrity Chili

Chili, being the great American favorite it is, has naturally drawn as aficionados some of the greats of show business, sports, and even politics. Here is a cross section of American celebrities' favorite chili recipes—from Hollywood's James Garner to Nashville's Chet Atkins, from Washington's Senator John Tower (whose blend is as fiery as his oratory) to auto racing's A. J. Foyt (with a side step to racing's first lady, Janet Guthrie). There was even to be a chili concocted by a legislative committee (well, not exactly—that sort of effort might be disastrous). But there was an Oklahoma legislative chili cookoff a few years back; and, you guessed it, the winning recipe was tabled somewhere along the way to this cookbook.

Perry Como's Favorite Chili

2 tablespoons salad oil
1 medium-sized onion, chopped
1 clove garlic, crushed
1 pound ground round
2 teaspoons salt
1 teaspoon paprika
2 teaspoons chili powder
2 16-ounce cans kidney beans
½ cup bean liquid
16-ounce can seasoned stewed tomatoes
6-ounce can tomato paste
½ teaspoon sugar
¾ teaspoon Tabasco sauce
12-ounce can whole kernel corn, drained

Heat oil in large skillet; add onion and garlic and cook until yellow, but not brown. Add beef; sprinkle with salt, paprika, and chili powder. Cook meat until brown, breaking up with fork. Drain kidney beans. Stir in bean liquid (½ cup), tomatoes, tomato paste, sugar, and Tabasco. Cover and simmer 30 minutes. Add kidney beans and corn; simmer 15 minutes, stirring occasionally.
Serves: 6.

Tom T. Hall's Fox Hollow Chili

1 pound ground beef
2 bell peppers
½ stalk celery
2 onions
2 cans red kidney beans
2 cans tomato puree
1 can jalapeño bean dip
Salt
Pepper

Brown beef in skillet. Chop vegetables finely. Transfer beef, vegetables, and all other ingredients to large pot and simmer for 2 hours. Add water for desired consistency; salt and pepper to taste.
Serves: 4.

Phil Harris's "That's What I Like About the South" Chili

5 pounds ground beef
½ pound ground suet
1 large onion, chopped
2 cloves garlic, minced
1 quart water
2 tablespoons cumin powder
⅓ cup chili powder
1 teaspoon honey
1 teaspoon red pepper powder
2 teaspoons salt

Boil beef, suet, onion, and garlic in 1 quart water for 20 minutes. Add remaining ingredients, cover, and simmer for 2 hours or more.
Serves: 8 to 10.

Peter Marshall's Hollywood Squares Chili

5 tablespoons chili powder
1 teaspoon cumin powder
1 teaspoon oregano
2 teaspoons celery salt
1 tablespoon paprika
1 tablespoon masa flour
1 teaspoon sugar
1 small bottle of soda water (about 10 oz.)
oil or rendered suet
3 pounds beef chuck, cut in small squares
4 tomatoes, peeled, deseeded, and cut in small squares
5 cloves garlic, cut in very small squares
1 jalapeño pepper, cut in very small squares
   (no veins or seeds)
1 No. 2 can tomato sauce
1 can beef broth
4 medium-sized white onions, cut in small squares
2 red bell peppers, cut in small squares

First mix the chili powder, cumin, oregano, celery salt, paprika, masa flour, and sugar with the soda water. Allow to stand while you are preparing the meat.

Brown beef in enough oil or rendered suet to keep it from sticking. Remove from skillet to a large pot. Add tomatoes, garlic, jalapeños, tomato sauce, beef broth, and spice mixture.

Cover and cook on a low boil for about 1 hour, stirring occasionally.

Add the chopped peppers and onions and simmer uncovered for 1 to 2 hours until meat is at the desired tenderness.

Add salt to taste.

Serves: 6 to 8.

James Garner's Oklahoma Chili

Known in Oklahoma as "sooner" chili.

>   3 pounds ground chuck
>   2 medium-sized onions, chopped
>   2 bell peppers, chopped
>   2 hot, yellow peppers, chopped
>   2 16-ounce cans whole tomatoes, chopped
>   ½ teaspoon garlic salt
>   2 teaspoons salt
>   ½ teaspoon black pepper
>   4 teaspoons chili powder
>   2 teaspoons brown sugar
>   ½ cup honey
>   ¼ pound margarine
>   1 teaspoon Tabasco sauce

Brown meat lightly in skillet and transfer to a large pot. Sauté onions and peppers in skillet and add them to meat. Sauté tomatoes and add to meat mixture. Add seasonings and blend well. Simmer for 3 hours in covered pot, stirring often.
Serves: 6 to 8.

Johnny Rutherford's Lone Star J. R. Chili

¼ cup cooking oil
2 cups chopped onions
1 cup celery, chopped
2 cups chopped green, sweet peppers
2 cloves garlic, minced
4 pounds lean beef, coarsely ground
4-ounce can diced green chiles
29-ounce can tomato puree
12-ounce can tomato paste
½ cup corn syrup
4 tablespoons chili powder
1 tablespoon paprika
2 tablespoons wine vinegar
1 teaspoon ground white pepper
1 teaspoon Tabasco sauce
Salt to taste
14-ounce can beef broth

To cooking oil, in a large skillet, add onions, celery, peppers, and garlic; sauté until tender. Set aside. In large kettle, add meat and brown; drain off fat, add onion, celery, pepper, garlic mixture and remaining ingredients (including sautéed onions, peppers, and garlic). Cover. Cook 3 hours, stirring often, over low heat.
Serves 12.

Joanne Dru's Red River Chili

First mix 1 can Diet Pepsi or Pepsi Light with the following:

> **9 tablespoons chili powder**
> **1 tablespoon oregano powder**
> **1 tablespoon granulated sugar**
> **1 tablespoon ground white pepper**
> **1 tablespoon salt**
> **½ teaspoon cilantro powder**

Allow to set while doing the following: **Dice:**

> **5 onions**
> **2 green bell peppers**
> **6 cloves garlic**

Heat in skillet with a little oil or rendered kidney suet until onions start to get transparent. Remove to a large pot.

Brown 4 pounds of round or flank steak cut in small cubes or coarse ground in the skillet with a small amount of cooking oil or rendered kidney suet and add to the pot.

Then add the mixed spices with two 12-ounce cans of tomato sauce and one 12-ounce can of water to the pot.

Simmer for 2 to 3 hours, uncovered, stirring every once and a while with a wooden spoon.

When meat has reached the desired tenderness, add salt to taste and remove from heat.

Let stand for at least 2 hours, then reheat or refrigerate until ready to use.

After reheating add juice of 1 lime.

Some of my friends like it with grated cheese and chopped onion—you may want to try it this way.

Serves: 8 to 10.

Minnie Pearl's Grinder Switch Chili

2 pounds ground chuck
1 large onion, chopped
2 medium-sized bell peppers, chopped
6 medium-sized tomatoes, chopped
2 cloves garlic, minced
6 jalapeño peppers, chopped
1 teaspoon salt
6 tablespoons chili powder
2 4-ounce cans diced green chiles
16-ounce can pinto beans, drained

Brown meat in large skillet, crumbling it apart with fork. Drain. Add onion, peppers, tomatoes, and garlic and cook until tender. Stir in remaining ingredients except beans. Cover and simmer for 1 hour, stirring often. Add beans and simmer, uncovered, for 25 minutes. *Serves: 6.*

Larry Mahan's Rodeo Chili

3 pounds beef, cut into ¼-inch cubes
6 cups water
4 cloves garlic, minced
½ teaspoon cayenne
3-ounce bottle chili powder
1 teaspoon oregano
1 tablespoon brown sugar
1 bay leaf
6 large tomatoes, chopped
12-ounce can tomato paste

Brown beef thoroughly; add remaining ingredients, blending well as they are added, and cook over low flame for 4 hours, stirring often.
Serves: 6 to 8.

Parnelli Jones's Off-Road Chili

28-ounce can whole tomatoes and juice, chopped
24-ounce can tomato juice
4-ounce can diced green chiles
3 medium-sized onions, chopped
2 medium-sized green, sweet peppers, chopped
1 can beer
6 tablespoons chili powder
1 teaspoon garlic powder
1 teaspoon seasoning salt
3 tablespoons sugar
6 jalapeño peppers, chopped
3 pounds pork shoulder, cut into ¼-inch cubes
3 pounds beef, cut into ¼-inch cubes
2 cups water

Place first 11 ingredients into heavy saucepan and simmer. Cook pork and beef in large skillet until redness is gone; drain fat. Add meat and chili powder to simmering sauce in saucepan and cook over low flame for 2 hours, stirring often. Add water during cooking if necessary.
Serves: 8.

Pete Fountain's Half-Fast Chili

1½ pounds lean beef shoulder, cut into 1-inch cubes
2 tablespoons oil
1 cup chopped onions
1 clove garlic, minced
1½ teaspoons salt
1 tablespoon paprika
6-ounce can tomato paste
12 ounces water
7-ounce can green chiles, chopped
16-ounce can pinto beans
10½-ounce can condensed onion soup
½ teaspoon cumin powder
1 tablespoon chili powder

Brown beef cubes in oil until seared on all sides. Add onions, garlic, salt, and paprika, turning meat and onions until onions are tender. Combine tomato paste and water until smooth. Add to beef mixture. Cook for 30 minutes with the lid on. Add chiles, pinto beans, onion soup, cumin, and chili powder. Cover and simmer, stirring often, for 1 hour.
Serves: 4 to 6.

Mom Unser's Ortega Green Chile Chili

1 pound lean pork shoulder, cut into ¼-inch cubes
2 tablespoons flour
2 tablespoons lard
½ cup chopped onions
1 clove garlic, minced
16-ounce can tomatoes, chopped
2 7-ounce cans Ortega brand diced green chiles
¼ teaspoon oregano
2½ teaspoons salt
2 cups water

Dredge meat in flour. Melt lard in a large skillet. Brown meat thoroughly. Add onion and garlic and cook until onion is tender. Add remaining ingredients. Simmer, covered, 1 to 2 hours, stirring occasionally. Remove cover. Simmer, uncovered, 5 to 10 minutes to desired consistency.
Serves: 4 to 6.

Charlie Dressen's Almost Chili

When California Angels General Manager E. J. (Buzzie) Bavasi was GM for the old Brooklyn Dodgers, his field manager, the late Charlie Dressen, fancied himself a chili expert. Chili lover Bavasi asked for his recipe.

Charlie wrote this in longhand for me when he managed my 1951 Brooklyn club.

"I don't know much about recipes, but I know there is an ingredient missing—I think it's chili," Buzzie laughed. And here's why:

> 2 medium-sized onions
> 4 cans tomatoes
> 4 cans beans
> 1 bunch celery
> 1 green pepper
> 3 pounds meat

Chop onions, celery, and green pepper very fine. Cook onions, celery, and green pepper about 45 minutes then add tomatoes. Cook about 15 minutes. Brown your meat, then in a few minutes add beans. If you like it hot, add pepper to taste.

When cooking onions, celery, and green peppers, add about a quart of water.

AUTHORS' NOTE: But he was great at baseball.

Carroll Shelby's Chili

1 pound round steak (coarse ground beef may be
    substituted for steak in like amounts)
1 pound chuck steak
Suet or ½ cup oil
8-ounce can tomato sauce
1 can beer
¼ cup ground dried No. 6 chile pepper
1½ teaspoons minced garlic
1 teaspoon chopped onions
1¼ teaspoon dried oregano
Scant ½ teaspoon paprika
1¼ teaspoon salt
1 teaspoon cumin powder
1 teaspoon cayenne, or to taste
¾ pound goat cheese, grated
½ teaspoon cumin seed

Sear meat in oil until brown. Place into a 2-quart iron
pot. Add tomato sauce and beer to meat. Add chile
pepper, garlic, onion, oregano, paprika, salt, and cumin
powder to meat. Simmer 1 hour. Stir but leave the lid on
as much as possible. Add cayenne, a pinch to 1 teaspoon,
simmer 2 more hours, stirring often. Add goat cheese
and cumin seed, stir while cooking another 30 minutes.
Serve pinto beans, chopped onions, and grated Cheddar
cheese separately so the "chili gourmet" can customize
the chili to his or her own taste.
Serves: 4 to 6.

Les McCann's Bandstand Chili

½ pound bacon
2 large onions, minced
2 cloves garlic, minced
2½ pounds ground beef
6-ounce can tomato paste
10-ounce can tomato sauce
8-ounce can tomatoes, chopped
3 tablespoons chili powder
¼ teaspoon cayenne
1 teaspoon salt
2 16-ounce cans kidney beans
1 bay leaf

Fry bacon, onions, and garlic in a heavy skillet until onions are tender. Crumble bacon and add beef. Brown well. Transfer to a large pot. Add remaining ingredients to pot and stir. Cover and simmer for 3 hours.
Serves: 6 to 8.

A. J. Foyt's 500-Mile Chili

3 pounds stewing beef, cubed
1 pound chorizo (Spanish sausage)
2 large onions, diced
5 cloves garlic, minced
3 large jalapeño peppers, peeled and diced
3 tablespoons olive oil
½ teaspoon cayenne
3 tablespoons chili powder
3 15-ounce cans tomato sauce
1 teaspoon salt
1½ cups water
1 bottle Mexican beer

Brown meat, onions, garlic, and jalapeños together in olive oil. While meat mixture is browning, add cayenne and chili powder. Stir often. Add tomato sauce, salt, water, and beer. Cover and cook on low heat for 30 minutes, stirring often. Uncover and simmer for 2 hours. *Serves: 6 to 8.*

Craig Claiborne's Chili

5 pounds lean chuck roast, cut into 1-inch cubes
½ cup olive oil
½ cup flour
½ cup chili powder, more or less to taste
2 teaspoons cumin seed
2 teaspoons dried oregano
6 to 10 cloves garlic, finely minced
4 cups fresh or canned beef broth
Salt
Freshly ground black pepper
Pinto beans (optional)

Pinto Beans: 1 pound dried pink or pinto beans
1 large onion, chopped
½ pound chunk salt pork
Salt

Trim and cube meat. Heat olive oil in a deep kettle and add cubed meat. Cook, stirring, until meat loses its red color. Sift together flour and chili powder. Sprinkle over meat, coating each piece evenly. Place the cumin and oregano in the palm of one hand. Rub the spices between the palms, sprinkling over the meat. Add the garlic and stir. Add the broth, stirring the meat constantly. Add salt and pepper and bring to a boil. Partly cover and simmer 3 to 4 hours or until the meat almost falls apart. If necessary, add more broth as the meat cooks. This chili should not be soupy, however. Serve with pinto beans if desired.

To prepare pinto beans, soak in water to cover for about 1 hour, then drain them. Cover again with water, about 2 inches above the beans, add the onion and salt pork and simmer until the beans are tender, about 2 hours. Add salt to taste.

Serves: 10 to 12.

Chet Atkins's Clinch Mountain Chili

        3 tablespoons instant minced onions
        1 teaspoon instant minced garlic
        3 tablespoons water
        3 tablespoons salad oil
        1½ pounds lean ground beef
        16-ounce can tomatoes, chopped
        2½ tablespoons chili powder
        1½ teaspoons salt
        14½-ounce can pinto or pink beans

Combine minced onion with minced garlic in a small bowl with water to rehydrate. Heat oil in a large skillet. Add onion and garlic, sauté 2 minutes. Add beef and brown. Blend in tomatoes, chili powder, and salt. Boil. Reduce heat to simmer and cook, uncovered, 10 minutes. Serve with pinto beans or pink beans.
Serves: 4 to 6.

Senator John Tower's Texas Chili

3 pounds chili meat
15-ounce can tomato sauce
1 cup water
1 teaspoon Tabasco sauce
3 heaping tablespoons chili powder or ground chile peppers
1 heaping tablespoon oregano
1 heaping teaspoon *comino* powder
2 onions, chopped
Garlic to taste
1 teaspoon salt
1 teaspoon cayenne
1 teaspoon paprika
12 red peppers
4 or 5 chile pods
2 heaping tablespoons flour

Sear meat until gray. Add tomato sauce and water, stirring until well blended. Add Tabasco, heaping tablespoons of chili powder, oregano, *comino* powder, onions, garlic, salt, cayenne, paprika, red peppers, and chile pods. Simmer 1 hour and 15 minutes over a fire of mesquite wood (if possible). Add thickening of 2 heaping tablespoons flour mixed with water. Simmer additional 30 minutes, stirring often.
Serves: 6 to 8.

Betty Ford's Chili

1 pound dried red beans
3 tablespoons shortening
4 tablespoons chili powder
Salt to taste
2 medium-sized onions, chopped
Shortening for frying
1½ pounds ground round of beef

Soak red beans overnight. Cook them in unsalted water until soft. Add shortening and 2 tablespoons chili powder. Salt to taste. Fry onions with shortening until soft. Add ground beef, remaining chili powder, and salt to taste. Stir until the meat is seared. Cover with water and cook slowly until done. Then add the meat mixture to the red beans and simmer a few minutes longer, to blend well.
Serves: 4 to 6.

Mrs. Tom Bradley's Chili

3 tablespoons oil (preferably safflower or soy oil)
2 medium-sized onions, chopped
2 green peppers, chopped
1 clove garlic, minced
2 pounds freshly ground round of beef
4 to 6 tablespoons chili powder
2 cans whole tomatoes
2 cloves
1 bay leaf
¼ teaspoon paprika
2 tablespoons cumin powder
6-ounce can tomato sauce
2 20-ounce cans kidney beans, drained

Heat oil and sauté onions, peppers, and garlic. Add beef, cook until crumbled. Add half the chili powder while these ingredients are browning. Simmer tomatoes in a large pot. Add spices, tomato sauce, and beans. Combine all ingredients and cook until thickened. Serve hot bowls of chili with fresh green salad and garlic toast. Don't forget to supply a bowl of freshly chopped onions for those who wish to sprinkle it on top of the chili.
Serves: 4 to 6.

The Favorite Chili of Rosalyn Carter

1 pound round steak, cut into bite-sized cubes
3 tablespoons oil
4-ounce can green chiles, chopped
8-ounce can tomato paste
1 small onion, chopped
1½ cups water
3 cloves garlic, minced
½ teaspoon cumin powder
½ teaspoon oregano
¼ teaspoon pepper (approximately)
1½ teaspoon sugar
4½ teaspoons flour
1½ teaspoons salt
2 tablespoons chili powder

Cook meat in hot oil until gray. Add the remaining ingredients. Simmer in a heavy pot or electric skillet about 1 hour, or until meat is tender.
Serves: 4 to 6.

Janet Guthrie's Indianapolis Chili

2 pounds pork sausage, ground
2 pounds ground beef
3 medium-sized onions, minced
⅔ cup chopped green peppers
4-ounce can green chiles, chopped
6 medium-sized mushrooms, sliced
4 large tomatoes, peeled and chopped
4 6-ounce cans tomato paste
4 15½-ounce cans beef consommé
3 16-ounce cans refried beans
1 teaspoon Tabasco sauce
1 teaspoon celery seed
½ teaspoon grated lemon rind
½ teaspoon pepper
2 teaspoons oregano leaves
2½-ounce-can chili powder
Salt to taste

Brown sausage, beef, onions, and green peppers in a large skillet, a little at a time. Place browned meats, vegetables, and spices in a large pot. Add the chiles and remaining ingredients to the pot and stir until all are well blended. Cook 2 hours, covered, stirring often to prevent sticking.
Serves: 8.

Walter McIlhenny's Favorite Chili

3 pounds lean stew beef, cut into 1-inch cubes,
    well trimmed
¼ cup salad oil
1 cup chopped onions
3 cloves garlic, minced
4 to 6 tablespoons chili powder
2 teaspoons salt
2 teaspoons cumin powder
2 teaspoons Tabasco sauce
4-ounce can green chiles, seeded and chopped
1 quart water
¼ cup chopped onions

Brown beef with oil in a large skillet. Add remaining
ingredients and mix well. Bring to a boil, reduce heat,
and simmer, uncovered, 1½ to 2 hours until meat is
tender. Garnish with chopped onion. If desired, serve
with additional pepper sauce.
Serves: 6 to 8.

Festus's (Ken Curtis) Gunsmoke Chili

4 pounds coarse ground venison or lean beef
2 large onions, minced
2 teaspoons monosodium glutamate
1½ teaspoons salt
1 teaspoon ground black pepper
2 tablespoons parsley flakes
1 teaspoon season all
1½ teaspoons basil leaves, crushed by hand
1½ teaspoons oregano leaves, crushed by hand
1 teaspoon cayenne
4 tablespoons chili powder
4 cups bouillon
4 cups tomato sauce

Mince the meat fine with a fork while browning. Add remaining ingredients in a large iron pot. Stir all together and simmer for 2½ to 3 hours.
Serves: 8 to 10.

Lady Bird Johnson's Pedernales River Special Chili

4 pounds chopped chili meat, venison or beef
1 large onion, chopped
2 cloves garlic, minced
1 teaspoon oregano
1 teaspoon cumin powder
2 tablespoons chili powder (more if you like it hotter)
2 12-ounce cans tomatoes
Salt to taste
2 cups hot water

Put meat, onion, and garlic into a large skillet and sear until lightly browned. Add all other ingredients. Bring to a boil. Lower heat, cover, and simmer 1 hour. Skim off grease and serve hot.
Serves: 8 to 10.

Chili's Cousins

Many dishes seem to have sprung *from* chili; many more simply came to resemble it—a family resemblance, if you will. There are even regional dishes throughout the country that people in those sections, perish the thought, *prefer* to chili. But whatever the dish, it certainly could be considered a chili *cousin*. These distant relatives can be enjoyed with or without chili on the menu.

Chili Pizza

2 pizza crusts, prepared
16-ounce can chili, with or without beans, divided in half
1 cup chopped green peppers, divided in half
1 cup chopped red peppers, divided in half
1 cup sliced mushrooms, divided in half

1 large onion, sliced and divided in half
2 cups shredded Mozzarella cheese, divided in half

Spread chili in equal amounts over each pizza crust. Spread remaining ingredients in equal amounts over pizzas and top with cheese. Place pizzas on rack in a preheated 425° F oven for 8 to 10 minutes.
Serves: 4 to 6.

Chili Joes

2 tablespoons chili powder
3 tablespoons butter
½ cup chopped green peppers
½ cup chopped celery
1 teaspoon celery seed
1 medium-sized onion, chopped
2 teaspoons prepared mustard
2 teaspoons pickled relish
1 pound ground beef
6-ounce can tomato paste
4 to 6 buns
1 cup shredded sharp Cheddar cheese
½ cup green onion tops (optional)

Combine chili powder, butter, green pepper, celery, celery seed, onion, mustard, and relish in a large bowl; stir to blend well. In a skillet, brown beef until it turns gray. Add tomato paste plus 1 can water; blend well. Add chili powder mixture a little at a time until well blended. Adjust liquids if too thick; cover and simmer 35 minutes; stir often. Toast buns. Spoon Chili Joe mixture over bun and sprinkle with cheese and top with chopped green onion tops. Repeat.
Serves: 4 to 6.

Chili Hash

If there's any chili left over . . .

4 to 6 servings leftover chili
1 large onion, chopped and cooked
2 medium-sized carrots, chopped and cooked
2 medium-sized potatoes, peeled, diced, and cooked
2 tablespoons oil

Heat chili in a medium saucepan. Add cooked onion, carrots, potatoes, and oil; stir to blend well. Heat for 30 minutes.
Serves: 4 to 6.

Chili Lima Beans

1 pound dry lima beans
½ pound ham, cut into 1-inch cubes
1 large onion, chopped
10½-ounce can condensed tomato soup
1 tablespoon chili powder
1 tablespoon Worcestershire sauce
2 teaspoons salt
7-ounce can whole kernel corn, drained
1 quart water

Place beans in large saucepan; cover with water. Bring to a boil, cover, reduce heat, and simmer 1 hour. Add remaining ingredients, plus 1 cup water. Simmer 1 hour, stirring frequently. Add more water if necessary during cooking.
Serves: 6.

Green Chile and Rice

7-ounce can green chiles, chopped and drained
1 small green onion, chopped
2 cups cooked rice
¼ cup butter, melted
¼ cup beef broth
2 cups sour cream
¼ teaspoon garlic powder

Combine all ingredients in a medium saucepan and heat thoroughly. Cover and simmer for 10 minutes. Remove from heat and let stand with lid on for 5 minutes. Serve immediately.
Serves: 4 to 6.

Green Chile Egg Scramble

3 tablespoons butter
8 eggs, well beaten
3 tablespoons milk
4 drops Tabasco sauce
½ cup green chiles, chopped
Salt to taste
1 teaspoon paprika
1 cup sour cream

Heat butter in a heavy skillet. Combine eggs, milk, and Tabasco sauce, whip to blend well. Add chiles to eggs, stirring well. Pour into heated butter, cook like scrambled eggs. Sprinkle eggs with paprika and salt. Serve with a bowl of sour cream.
Serves: 4.

Chili Cheese Pie

4 to 6 servings of your favorite chili
⅔ cup cornmeal
1 cup flour
⅔ cup milk
2 teaspoons sugar
2 eggs
1 teaspoon cream of tartar
2 tablespoons butter, melted
2 cups diced Cheddar cheese

Pour chili into a 3-quart baking dish. Place dish in oven and bake at 375° F for 15 minutes. Mix cornmeal and flour in a small bowl. Combine milk, sugar, and eggs; beat until an even color. Add cream of tartar, butter, and Cheddar cheese to milk mixture and blend well. Remove chili from oven. Pour batter over chili and bake at 375° F for 30 minutes.
Serves: 4 to 6.

Chile-Potato-Chorizo Sauté

½ pound chorizo (Spanish sausage), thinly sliced
1 tablespoon oil
2 pounds potatoes, cooked, peeled, and sliced
1 large onion, sliced
2 4-ounce cans Ortega brand sliced green chiles
1 teaspoon salt

Lightly brown the sausage with oil in a large skillet. Add remaining ingredients. Cook, stirring, until heated thoroughly.
Serves: 4 to 6.

Chili Tuna-Noodle Casserole

7-ounce can tuna
10½-ounce can condensed cream of celery soup
2 cups cooked macaroni
2 tablespoons parsley flakes
2 teaspoons chili powder
3 tablespoons butter, melted
½ cup bread crumbs

Combine tuna, celery soup, macaroni, parsley flakes, and chili powder; blend thoroughly. Pour into a greased 1½-quart casserole. Pour melted butter over bread crumbs and toss gently in a small bowl. Sprinkle tuna with the bread crumbs. Bake in a preheated 350° F oven for 40 minutes.
Serves: 4 to 6.

Chili Bean Casserole

1 pound ground beef
1 tablespoon shortening
16-ounce can kidney beans, undrained
10½-ounce can cream of tomato soup
1 teaspoon salt
2 teaspoons chili powder
¼ cup instant minced onion

Brown meat in shortening. Add beans, undiluted cream of tomato soup, salt, chili powder, and instant minced onion. Mix well. Pour into a 1-quart casserole. Bake in a preheated 320° F oven for 40 minutes. Serve hot as the main dish.
Serves: 4.

Chili Steak-and-Eggs

4 teaspoons oil
4 tablespoons chili powder
2 teaspoons onion powder
½ teaspoon garlic powder
1 tablespoon seasoning salt
2 tablespoons flour
4 Porterhouse steaks
8 eggs
3 tablespoons butter
A-1 sauce

Warm oil and set aside. Combine chili powder, onion powder, garlic powder, seasoning salt, and flour until well blended. Pour equal amounts of oil on each steak, coating each side well. Dust one side with powdered mixture and pound into the steak. This can be done with a fork or the blunt side of a knife. Broil, grill, or pan-fry steaks to desired doneness. Fry eggs in butter. Serve steak-and-eggs with A-1 sauce for that Western taste! *Serves: 4.*

Chicken with Chili Sauce

2 pounds chicken, cut up
2 tablespoons oil
1 small onion, chopped
¼ teaspoon garlic, minced
1 can beef broth
16-ounce can tomatoes, chopped
1 package chili mix (any brand)

Brown chicken thoroughly in oil. While chicken is browning, add onion and garlic to beef broth in a small saucepan and simmer 20 minutes, covered. Place chicken in an ovenproof pan and bake at 375° F for 30 minutes. Add tomatoes to beef broth and break apart into small pieces. Add chili mix to tomatoes and beef broth; cover and simmer 20 minutes. Pour broth mixture over chicken, coating thoroughly. Bake 15 to 20 minutes at 350° F. Serve with rice.
Serves: 6.

Santa Fe Lima Bean Soup

¼ **cup instant minced onion**
¼ **teaspoon instant minced garlic**
3 quarts water
¼ **pound bacon, diced**
1 pound dried baby lima beans
4 teaspoons salt
¼ **teaspoon ground black pepper**
16-ounce can tomatoes, broken up
2 tablespoons brown sugar
2 tablespoons parsley flakes
1 tablespoon chili powder

Rehydrate minced onion and garlic in ¼ cup water for 10 minutes. Fry bacon until crisp in a heavy skillet. Remove bacon and set aside. Sauté onion and garlic in bacon drippings for 5 minutes. Remove from heat. Add remaining water, lima beans, salt, black pepper, and reserved bacon. Bring to a boil, then reduce heat, cover, and simmer 1½ to 2 hours or until beans are tender. Add tomatoes and brown sugar. Cover and simmer 1 hour or until beans are very soft. Stir in parsley flakes and chili powder. Cover and simmer 10 minutes longer.
Serves: 4 to 6.

Coney Sauce

The hot dog sauce.

> 2 tablespoons oil
> 1 pound ground beef
> 1 large onion, minced
> ½ clove garlic, minced
> 6-ounce can tomato paste
> 1 tablespoon chili powder
> 1 teaspoon Mexican oregano (available
>   at most epicurean shops)
> ½ teaspoon salt
> 1 teaspoon dry mustard
> 1 cup tomato juice
> ½ teaspoon celery salt

Heat oil in a heavy skillet and brown beef, onion, and garlic. Break apart until crumbly. Add tomato paste, chili powder, Mexican oregano, salt, and dry mustard. Stir to mix well. Break apart any large pieces of meat. Cook 30 minutes, stirring often. Add tomato juice and celery salt; stir, reduce heat to simmer, and cover for 1 hour or until mixture thickens.
Yield: About 2½ cups.

Chile Rice

> 4-ounce can chiles, chopped (reserve liquid)
> 1 stalk celery, minced
> 1 small onion, minced
> 2 tablespoons oil or butter
> 1 cup long grain rice

3 cups water
1 teaspoon salt
½ teaspoon pepper
1 small jar pimentos, chopped
½ green pepper, chopped
½ teaspoon oregano
½ teaspoon cumin powder

Combine chiles, celery, onion, and oil in a small saucepan, cover, and simmer 15 minutes. Combine rice, water, and salt in a medium saucepan, cook at medium heat, stirring occasionally, until water boils. Reduce heat to simmer and cover; cook 20 minutes. Add pepper, pimentos, green pepper, oregano, and cumin, stir to blend well. Simmer 10 minutes. Serve steaming hot.
Serves: 4 to 6.

Saucy Baked Chili Chicken

3 pound chicken, cut into serving pieces
10½-ounce can condensed cream of mushroom soup
½ soup can of milk
2 tablespoons instant minced onions
4 teaspoons chili powder
10½-ounce package frozen baby lima beans

Place chicken in a large shallow casserole, uncovered, in a preheated 350° F oven for 45 minutes.

Combine mushroom soup, milk, onions, chili powder, and lima beans in a saucepan. Bring to a boil; reduce heat. Cover and simmer 10 minutes.

Pour off chicken fat from casserole, spoon soup mixture over chicken. Bake, uncovered, 15 minutes, until chicken is tender.
Serves: 6 to 8.

Chili Burgers

2 tablespoons oil
3 pounds ground beef
1 medium-sized onion, chopped
1 clove garlic, minced
1 cup tomato sauce
4-ounce can green chiles, chopped
3 tablespoons chili powder
½ teaspoon salt
1 teaspoon Tabasco sauce
1 egg, beaten
4 tablespoons masa flour
½ teaspoon salt
½ teaspoon pepper
1 teaspoon cumin powder
Oil for frying
2 cups Monterey Jack cheese, shredded

Heat 2 tablespoons oil in a heavy skillet and brown 1 pound beef, onion, and garlic for 15 minutes. Add tomato sauce, green chiles, chili powder, salt, and Tabasco sauce; stir well to blend. Cook, uncovered, until mixture thickens, about 45 minutes over low heat. In a mixing bowl combine remaining 2 pounds beef, egg, masa flour, salt, pepper, and cumin. Mix with hands to blend well. Make 3-inch beef patties and place on a platter. Fill one patty with 2 to 3 tablespoons thickened chili and top with a second patty; pinch edges to seal in juices. Fry in hot oil on both sides. To serve, top with Monterey Jack cheese and remaining chili.
Serves: 8 to 10.

Chili Crepes

Filling:

  ½ pound ground chuck
  2 tablespoons oil
  ½ cup minced celery
  ½ cup minced onions
  ½ cup minced green peppers
  1 teaspoon minced garlic
  1 tablespoon chili powder
  1 large green chile, minced
  1 teaspoon salt
  2 drops Tabasco sauce
  6 stuffed green olives, chopped
  6-ounce can tomato paste
  6-ounce can water

Crepes: 3 eggs   ¼ teaspoon salt
         1 cup flour   2 cups milk
         1 cup cornmeal   ¼ cup oil

Brown ground chuck in oil until crumbly. Add minced vegetables and sauté until tender. Add chili powder, green chiles, salt, and Tabasco. Stir to blend well. Add olives, tomato paste, and water. Stir, cover, and simmer for 1 hour until thickened.

To make crepes:
Combine eggs, flour, cornmeal, and salt. Slowly add milk to the thickened mixture until smooth. Add oil until well blended. Chill at least 1 hour (while chili filling is simmering). Cook on an upside-down crepe griddle or in a traditional pan. This mixture will be thick; if a thinner batter is desired, thin with 1 or 2 tablespoons milk.
Yield: 30 crepes.

Chili Pie

1 tablespoon butter
1 medium-sized onion, sliced
2 tablespoons lard
1 pound beef, coarsely ground
1 medium-sized onion, chopped
1 small clove garlic, chopped
¼ cup green pepper
3 tablespoons chili powder
½ teaspoon salt
6 drops Tabasco sauce
6-ounce can tomato paste
16-ounce can refried beans
9-inch pie shell, uncooked
1 cup grated Cheddar cheese

Melt butter in medium skillet and sauté sliced onion until tender. Set aside. Melt lard in skillet and brown beef, chopped onion, garlic, green pepper, chili powder, salt, and Tabasco; stir. Add tomato paste plus 1 can water; blend well. Add a little more water if mixture is too thick. Cover and simmer 1 hour. While mixture is simmering, spread refried beans over bottom of unbaked pie shell. Pour thickened meat mixture over refried beans. Sprinkle sliced onions over chili mixture and top with grated Cheddar cheese. Place pie into a preheated 350° F oven for 40 to 50 minutes.
Serves: 4 to 6.

Chili Steak

3 pounds round steak
4 tablespoons flour

5 tablespoons oil
1 teaspoon salt
½ teaspoon pepper
3 medium-sized onions, cut in rings
3 tablespoons chili powder
6 drops Tabasco sauce
2 cans beef broth

Cut steak into serving sized pieces. Roll in flour, coating each piece well. In a heavy skillet, heat oil and fry steak until well browned on both sides. Salt and pepper steak as it is frying. Add onion rings and sprinkle with chili powder. Combine leftover flour, Tabasco, and beef broth, stir until all lumps dissolve. Pour over meat mixture, cover, and cook at low heat 1 hour, stirring frequently, or until meat is tender.
Serves: 6.

New Mexican Goulash

1 small onion, minced
1½ pounds ground beef
½ pound ground pork
16-ounce can tomatoes
5 to 6 carrots, thinly sliced
1 package prepared chili mix (any brand)
1 can beef broth

Combine onion, beef, and pork in a large bowl. Blend thoroughly and roll into small balls. Brown balls at low heat and place into a casserole. Combine tomatoes, carrots, beef broth, and chili mix until well blended. Pour tomato mixture over meatballs and bake at 350° F for 30 minutes.
Serves: 4 to 6.

Chili Soup

3 pounds hamburger
16-ounce can tomato sauce
2 10¾-ounce cans tomato soup
¼ teaspoon dehydrated minced garlic
2 tablespoons olive oil
2 medium-sized onions, chopped
4 tablespoons chili powder
¼ cup uncooked rice
1 teaspoon salt
3 shakes Tabasco sauce
¼ teaspoon pepper

Brown hamburger. Add tomato sauce, tomato soup, and garlic; stir to blend well. Heat olive oil in a heavy skillet; sauté onion until tender. Add onion to meat. Add chili powder, rice, salt, Tabasco, and pepper. Simmer for 1½ hours, stirring frequently to prevent sticking.
Serves: 6 to 8.

Chili Bean and Ham Soup

1 ham shank
4 cups water
¼ cup onion flakes
2 tablespoons mixed vegetable flakes
¼ teaspoon instant minced garlic
¼ teaspoon ground black pepper
2 16-ounce cans kidney beans
4 teaspoons chili powder

Place ham shank, water, onion flakes, vegetable flakes, garlic, and pepper into a large saucepan. Bring to a boil, then reduce heat. Cover and simmer 1½ hours or until ham is tender. Remove shank from broth. Cut meat from bone and dice. Add diced meat and kidney beans to broth. Cover and simmer 30 minutes. Stir in chili powder. Cover and simmer 10 minutes longer.
Serves: 4.

Stuffed Green Peppers

> 6 medium-sized green peppers
> 1 pound ground beef
> 1 tablespoon olive oil
> 1 medium-sized onion, minced
> 16-ounce can tomatoes, chopped
> ½ cup long grain rice
> 1 cup tomato juice
> 1½ teaspoons salt
> 1 tablespoon chili powder
> ¼ cup tomato paste
> ½ teaspoon Tabasco sauce

Soak green peppers in ice water for 30 minutes. Slice off tops and remove seeds. Drop chilled, deseeded green peppers into boiling water, enough to cover, for 5 minutes. Drain and set aside. Heat olive oil in a large skillet and add remaining ingredients, stirring well. Cover and cook 10 minutes, stirring often. Remove from heat. Fill peppers with meat mixture and place in a greased baking dish. Bake at 375° F for 1 hour and 15 minutes.
Serves: 6.

Chili Hominy Bake

1 pound pork, ground
1 small onion, minced
1 clove garlic, minced
2 20-ounce cans hominy, undrained
2 cups sour cream
2 ounces cream cheese
1½ cups provolone cheese
1 teaspoon salt
2 tablespoons chili powder
1 cup bread crumbs

Brown pork, onion, and garlic until meat crumbles. Add hominy, blending well. Add remaining ingredients except bread crumbs. Stir until cheese melts and blends thoroughly. Fold in bread crumbs. Pour into a greased 2-quart casserole. Preheat oven at 350° F for 10 minutes. Bake for 35 to 45 minutes or until top turns crusty brown.
Serves: 4 to 6.

Chili Meat Loaf

Perfect served with Vegetable Medley (see p. 171).

3 pounds ground beef
1 large onion, chopped
2 teaspoons salt
1 teaspoon Tabasco sauce
8-ounce can tomato sauce
4 tablespoons chili powder

**7-ounce can diced green chiles, drained
   and chopped very fine
3 eggs
½ cup cornmeal**

Mix with hands, beef, onion, salt, Tabasco, tomato sauce,
chili powder, green chiles, eggs, and cornmeal. Shape
into loaf in appropriate baking pan. Place in preheated
350° F oven for 1 hour.
Serves: 6.

Chile-Stuffed Cabbage

**8 large cabbage leaves
1 large onion, sliced
1 large clove garlic, minced
1 tablespoon butter or margarine
2 4-ounce cans Ortega brand sliced green chiles
1 cup cooked rice
1 cup shredded Monterey Jack cheese
½ teaspoon salt
½ teaspoon coriander
½ teaspoon oregano
7-ounce can Ortega brand green chile salsa**

Drop cabbage leaves in boiling water. Cook just until
leaves are limp. Drain. Cook onion and garlic in butter
until tender. Mix in chiles, rice, cheese, and seasonings.
Spoon chile filling on stem end of cabbage leaves. Fold in
sides and roll tightly. Place stem side down in a 6-by-10-
inch baking dish. Pour salsa over all. Bake, covered, in
preheated 350° F oven for 35 to 40 minutes or until hot
and bubbly.
Serves: 8.

Chili Meatballs

1½ pounds ground round steak
1 small onion, minced
1 clove garlic, minced
1 teaspoon parsley flakes
1 envelope dried onion soup mix
1 egg
16-ounce can refried beans
1 cup tomato juice
½ teaspoon Tabasco sauce
3 tablespoons chili powder
⅓ cup oil for frying

Combine all ingredients except oil in a large bowl; blend well. Roll meat into 1-inch balls. Heat oil in a large skillet and add as many meatballs as will fit into the pan without them touching one another while frying. Turn often to brown on all sides. Place cooked meatballs in a covered pan. Repeat until all are cooked.
Serves: 4 to 6.

And to Go with Chili...

Many chili cooks feel that chili itself is not enough; there should be something else served with it, either to tone down the main course or to enhance it—if it needs enhancing. Good chili cooks usually have a side dish or two up their aprons. Here is a selection of fifty recipes to choose from, dishes that will go nicely with chili—from Hush Puppies to Sombrero Chili Dip to Mississippi Cornpone; there are bean dishes, such as Vermont Lima Bean Casserole or the Cajun country favorite Red Beans and Rice, to serve on the side in case a purist is present, insisting that chili should *not include* beans. Also there is jalapeño griddle cakes, which has a similar heritage to chili itself. But whether it be the tangy Spanish omelet or the Texas delight, Pecos River Muffins, a chili party is always improved with the proper companion to the main course.

Breads

Mississippi Cornpone

1 cup flour
1 cup cornmeal
4 teaspoons baking powder
½ teaspoon salt
¼ cup molasses
1 egg
1 cup milk
¼ cup bacon drippings

Sift together flour, cornmeal, baking powder, and salt in a mixing bowl. Add molasses, egg, milk, and bacon drippings; beat until smooth. Bake in a well-greased 8-inch-square baking pan at 425° F for 20 to 25 minutes. *Serves: 8.*

Hush Puppies

1½ cups white cornmeal
½ cup unsifted all-purpose flour
1 teaspoon salt
1 teaspoon baking powder
½ teaspoon baking soda
¾ cup buttermilk
1 egg, beaten
½ teaspoon Tabasco sauce
16 ounces oil or lard

In medium bowl, mix cornmeal, flour, salt, baking powder, and baking soda. Stir in buttermilk, egg, and Tabasco; mix well. Drop by tablespoons into oil that has

been heated to 375° F in a deep fryer. Fry until light brown, about 2 to 3 minutes. Remove and drain on paper towels.
Yield: About 20 hush puppies.

Bran Muffins

1½ cup bran flakes (breakfast type)
¾ cup flour
1 tablespoon baking powder
¼ teaspoon salt
3 tablespoons sugar
1 egg, beaten
3 tablespoons shortening
¾ cup buttermilk

Combine dry ingredients; blend well. Combine egg, shortening, and buttermilk. Pour egg mixture into bran mixture; stir enough to moisten bran mixture. Do not beat. Spoon into greased muffin tins to fill ¾ full. Bake at 400° F for 20 minutes.
Yield: 12 muffins.

Corn Muffins

1 cup flour
1 cup cornmeal, yellow
4 teaspoons baking powder
4 tablespoons sugar
1 teaspoon salt
1 egg, beaten
1¼ cups milk
3 tablespoons shortening, melted

Sift all dry ingredients together in a large bowl. Combine egg with milk and shortening; pour into flour mixture and stir just enough to moisten flour mixture. Do not beat. Spoon into greased muffin tins to fill ¾ full. Bake at 400° F for 20 minutes.
Yield: 12 muffins.

Mild Jalapeño Cornbread

½ cup flour
1½ cups cornmeal
2 teaspoons sugar
1 teaspoon baking soda
1 teaspoon baking powder
1½ cups buttermilk
1 teaspoon salt
7-ounce can mild jalapeño peppers, chopped
1½ cups minced onions
2 eggs, beaten
1 cup sharp Cheddar cheese
3 tablespoons bacon drippings

Combine dry ingredients, except salt, in a large bowl. Heat milk with salt until hot. Add jalapeños and onion; cover and cook for 30 minutes over low heat. Cool. Combine eggs and Cheddar cheese. Blend dry ingredients, liquids, cheese mixture, and bacon drippings until smooth. Pour into a well-greased 9-inch-square baking pan. Bake in a preheated 425° F oven for 40 to 50 minutes.
Serves: 6.

Beer Pan Bread

4 cups Bisquick baking mix
1 teaspoon brown sugar
2 teaspoons sugar
12-ounce can beer
2 tablespoons grease

Combine Bisquick baking mix, sugars, and beer, stirring until thoroughly blended. Pour into a heavily greased iron skillet and cover. Simmer on top of the stove, covered, at low heat for 30 to 35 minutes. Slice while piping hot and serve like corn bread.
Serves: 6 to 8.

Cherokee County Cornbread

4 teaspoons baking powder
1 teaspoon salt
½ teaspoon baking soda
1 cup flour
2 cups cornmeal
2 cups buttermilk
3 eggs, beaten
1 tablespoon brown sugar
6 tablespoons bacon drippings
4-ounce can green chiles, chopped

Combine dry ingredients in a large bowl. Add buttermilk, eggs, brown sugar, and bacon drippings; stir. Fold in green chiles. Pour mixture into a large iron skillet that has been greased. Bake cornbread in preheated 400° F oven for 30 to 40 minutes.
Serves: 6 to 8.

Jalapeño Griddle Cakes

2 cups Bisquick baking mix
2 eggs
1 small green chile, seeded and chopped
¼ cup jalapeño peppers, minced
¾ cup buttermilk

Beat ingredients with a whisk in a small bowl until smooth. Pour small amounts onto hot griddle, about ¼ cup each, and cook until slightly thickened. Turn and cook until golden brown. Serve with butter and honey. *Yield: 12 griddle cakes.*

Pecos River Muffins

2½ teaspoons baking powder
⅔ cup all-purpose flour
½ teaspoon salt
1 cup whole wheat flour
1½ cups buttermilk
⅓ cup honey
½ cup oil
⅓ cup minced sunflower seeds

Combine baking powder, flour, salt, and wheat flour in a large bowl. In a small bowl combine buttermilk, honey, and oil. Add liquids to flour mixture, stirring until smooth. Fold in sunflower seeds. Pour mixture into greased muffin tins, filling them two thirds full. Bake in a preheated 400° F oven for 12 minutes. *Yield: 12 muffins.*

Buttermilk Biscuits

2 cups flour
1 teaspoon salt
1 teaspoon baking powder
5 tablespoons shortening
¾ cup buttermilk
½ teaspoon baking soda
3 tablespoons butter, melted

Combine flour, salt, and baking powder in a small bowl. Add shortening; blend with a fork until mixture is crumbly. Combine buttermilk and soda and add to flour mixture; blend until smooth. Place dough on a floured surface and roll ½-inch thick. Cut with a biscuit cutter and bake in a preheated 400° F oven for 10 minutes. Remove from oven and brush tops with butter and return to oven for 5 more minutes.
Yield: 20 biscuits.

Parsley Bread

¼ cup butter, softened
2 tablespoons finely chopped onions
Fresh parsley
¼ teaspoon Tabasco sauce
1 loaf French bread

Combine butter, onion, parsley, and Tabasco sauce in a small bowl. Cut bread into ½-inch slices. Spread bread on both sides with seasoned butter, reassemble bread into a loaf, and wrap in heavy-duty foil. Bake at 375° F for 15 to 20 minutes, or until hot.
Serves: 6 to 8.

Louisiana French Toast

A perfect companion for breakfast chili.

> 2 eggs
> ¼ cup canned milk
> 1 tablespoon sugar
> ½ teaspoon salt
> ¼ teaspoon Tabasco sauce
> Butter
> 6 slices French bread, sliced diagonally

Beat eggs with fork in shallow dish; stir in milk, sugar, salt, and Tabasco sauce. Melt a little butter in a skillet. Quickly dip bread slices, one at a time, into egg mixture; turn until well coated. Brown on both sides in skillet. *Serves: 6.*

Main Dishes

Chili and Dumplings

> 4 to 6 servings of your favorite chili
> 2 cups Bisquick baking mix
> ⅔ cup milk

Heat chili in a large pot to near boiling. Combine baking mix and milk until a soft dough forms. Drop by spoonfuls onto hot chili. Simmer at low heat, uncovered, for 10 minutes. Cover and cook 10 minutes. *Yield: 12 dumplings.*

Arizona-Style Macaroni

4 cups cooked macaroni (prepared according to package
   directions)
¾ cup mayonnaise
¼ cup cider vinegar
1 tablespoon prepared mustard
1 teaspoon salt
½ teaspoon pepper
¼ cup green onion tops
½ cup minced celery
¼ cup minced onions
3 eggs, hard boiled
¼ cup green peppers, minced

While macaroni is cooking, combine mayonnaise with
vinegar, mustard, salt, and pepper, blending until
smooth. Add onion tops, celery, onions, 2 chopped hard-
boiled eggs, and green pepper. Drain macaroni and cool
slightly. Combine mayonnaise mixture with macaroni
and toss to blend well. Garnish with wedges of hard-
boiled egg.
Serves: 6.

Country Omelet

An omelet with a different taste.

3 tablespoons butter
1 small onion, chopped
2 medium-sized potatoes, cooked and diced
¾ cup cooked ham, diced

Salt to taste
6 eggs
3 tablespoons water
½ teaspoon Tabasco sauce
2 tablespoons grated Parmesan cheese

Melt 1 tablespoon butter in heavy skillet. Add onion and cook until tender. Stir in potatoes and ham; sprinkle salt over mixture and cook until heated. Slightly beat eggs with water and Tabasco; pour into skillet. When eggs begin to set, sprinkle with cheese and add remaining 2 tablespoons butter at one side. Tip pan to spread butter and shake gently. When eggs are set, use a spatula and turn the omelet over to brown the other side. Fold and serve.
Serves: 4.

Campfire Baked Beans

Would make even a Texan happy if served with chili.

¼ cup brown sugar
2 teaspoons prepared mustard
¼ teaspoon Tabasco sauce
¼ teaspoon salt
2 16-ounce cans baked beans

Combine brown sugar, mustard, Tabasco, and salt in saucepan. Stir in baked beans and place over low heat and cook for 25 minutes, stirring occasionally.
Serves: 6.

Red Beans and Rice

1 pound dried dark beans (if unavailable,
   substitute kidney beans)
½ pound lean salt pork, diced
1 garlic clove, minced
2 tablespoons chopped parsley
1 teaspoon salt
½ teaspoon Tabasco sauce
4 cups hot cooked rice

In large saucepan, cover dried beans with water and
soak overnight. Simmer, covered, until tender, about 2
hours, adding additional water if necessary. Drain. In
small skillet, fry salt pork until crisp and brown.
Remove pork and reserve. Pour off about half of fat and
add garlic to skillet. Cook 2 to 3 minutes. Add to drained
beans with parsley, salt, Tabasco, and reserved salt
pork. Heat and serve over rice.
Serves: 8.

Baked Pinto Beans

1 pound dried pinto beans
6 strips bacon, chopped
1 large onion, chopped
1 cup brown sugar
½ teaspoon Tabasco sauce
1 tablespoon Worcestershire sauce
½ teaspoon salt
2 teaspoons dry mustard
½ teaspoon celery seed
2 cups ketchup

Wash beans, cover with water, and soak overnight. Rinse beans and place in an ovenproof dish or crock. Fry bacon with onion until onion is tender and bacon is crisp. Add bacon-onion mixture to crock. Add remaining ingredients to crock; stir well. Bake beans at 350° F for 2½ to 3 hours; check beans often and add a little liquid if beans appear too dry. Keep crock tightly covered while baking. *Serves: 6 to 8.*

Spanish Omelet

3 medium-sized onions, thinly sliced
2 green peppers, thinly sliced and seeded
3 to 4 tablespoons olive oil
1 teaspoon chili powder
½ teaspoon salt
½ teaspoon pepper
½ teaspoon Tabasco sauce
1 bay leaf
½ teaspoon oregano
8 eggs, beaten
4 tablespoons milk

Sauté onions and green peppers in olive oil in a heavy skillet until tender. Sprinkle chili powder, salt, pepper, Tabasco sauce, bay leaf, and oregano over sautéed vegetables. Toss to blend. Simmer, stirring frequently, 5 minutes. Remove bay leaf and discard. Beat eggs with milk in a large bowl. Pour eggs over vegetables, being very careful to keep vegetables in the center as much as possible. Turn only once and serve.
Serves: 4.

Refried Bean Pie

If there's a Texan around, you can't put the beans in the chili, so . . .

>   2 cups refried beans
>   2 eggs, beaten
>   2 cups sugar
>   2 tablespoons pumpkin pie spices
>   1 teaspoon vanilla
>   1 teaspoon cornstarch
>   1 unbaked 9-inch pie shell

Heat refried beans in a medium saucepan. Slowly add eggs, then the sugar to beans; blend. Add spices, vanilla, and cornstarch; stir until well blended. Cool 30 minutes. Fill pastry shell and bake in a preheated 375° F oven for 1 hour.
Yield: 9-inch pie. Serves: 4.

Vegetables

Summer Squash with Green Chiles

>   2 7-ounce cans green chiles, chopped
>   2 medium-sized summer squash, cubed
>   2 tablespoons butter
>   1 teaspoon salt

Combine all ingredients in a deep saucepan and simmer until tender. Add a little water if necessary.
Serves: 6.

Old-Fashioned Cucumbers

8 to 12 medium-sized cucumbers
4 tablespoons salt
3 cups white vinegar
8 tablespoons sugar
1 teaspoon pepper

Wash and cut cucumbers into paper-thin slices; place in deep bowl; sprinkle with salt. Let stand covered for 2 hours. Drain; press out remaining liquid. Stir in remaining ingredients and refrigerate for 4 hours.
Serves: 6.

Pickled Okra

2 cups cider vinegar
2 cups water
1 tablespoon salt
2 tablespoons mustard seed
2 tablespoons dill seed
2 tablespoons celery seed
½ teaspoon Tabasco sauce
1 pound fresh okra
2 cloves garlic

In large kettle, combine vinegar, water, salt, mustard seed, dill seed, celery seed, and Tabasco. Simmer 10 minutes.

Cut stem ends off okra and place in 2 sterilized 12-ounce jars. Add a garlic clove to each jar; fill with pickling liquid. Seal and store at least 3 weeks.
Yield: 2 12-ounce jars.

Vegetable Medley

16-ounce can whole kernel corn, drained
16-ounce can peas, drained
1 large tomato, diced
3 tablespoons butter
1 teaspoon salt
½ teaspoon Tabasco sauce

Combine corn, peas, tomato, butter, salt, and Tabasco sauce in saucepan and heat to serving temperature. *Serves: 6.*

Vegetable medley can also be added directly to baking pan with Chili Meat Loaf (see page 154).

Zucchini Salsa Bake

3 medium-sized zucchini squash (2½ to 3 pounds)
Butter
2 7-ounce cans Ortega brand green chile salsa
Salt, pepper, and garlic to taste

Wash squash and cut off ends. Slice lengthwise. Place, cut side up, in a buttered 8-by-13-inch baking dish. Pour salsa over squash and cover dish. Bake in a preheated 350° F oven for 30 minutes. Remove cover, add salt, pepper, and garlic salt to taste. Continue to bake, uncovered, for another 15 minutes, if needed. Test by piercing with a fork: Squash should be soft but not mushy. Serve hot. *Serves: 6.*

Vegetables Veracruz

½ pound cherry tomatoes
2 4-ounce cans Ortega brand sliced green chiles
¼ cup ripe olives, pitted and sliced
½ teaspoon salt
¼ teaspoon basil
1 tablespoon olive oil
Parmesan cheese (optional)

Place tomatoes and chiles in a 1-quart casserole dish. Sprinkle with remaining ingredients, except cheese. Bake in preheated 450° F oven 10 minutes. Top with Parmesan cheese if desired.
Serves: 6.

Vermont Lima Bean Casserole

1 pound dried lima beans
5 cups water
1 large onion, studded with 8 whole cloves
½ cup maple syrup
½ cup ketchup
2 teaspoons salt
1 bay leaf
½ pound salt pork, thinly sliced
1 teaspoon Tabasco sauce

Rinse beans and soak overnight. Add onion, bring to a boil (using water in which beans have soaked), and boil, uncovered, for 5 minutes. Pour into 3-quart casserole without draining. Add remaining ingredients and cover; bake in preheated 325° F oven for 3 hours, or until beans are tender.
Serves: 8.

Mexican Corn

2 10-ounce packages frozen corn
1 tablespoon olive oil
2 tablespoons butter
1 medium-sized onion, minced
2 cups tomato sauce
4 ounces green chiles, chopped
1 teaspoon salt
¼ teaspoon pepper
1 tablespoon pimento (optional)

Place frozen corn in a deep saucepan and heat over medium flame. Add remaining ingredients, cover pan, reduce heat to simmer, and cook 1 hour, stirring frequently.
Serves: 6.

Watermelon Fruit Bowl

A perfect start or finish for any chili gathering.

1 watermelon
1 quart rum
2 small cantaloupes
2 small honeydew melons
4 cups pineapple chunks
4 cups pitted sweet cherries or strawberries
Fresh mint for garnish

Cut a horizontal slice off the watermelon. Scoop meat out of melon to within 2 inches from bottom to form bowl. Remove seeds from melon and cut into bite-sized pieces.

Cut large scallops around edge of melon bowl; cover and chill. Peel and seed other melons; cut into bite-sized pieces. Combine fruits. Place melon on a serving plate and pour rum into melon bowl. Mix fruit into rum. Garnish with mint.

Serves: 8.

Salads

Indian Summer Salad

2 16-ounce cans whole kernel corn, drained
1 cup sliced celery
1 cup diced tomatoes
¼ cup chopped green peppers
1 sprig fresh dill, minced
  (or ½ teaspoon dried dill)

Avery Island Dressing:
              ¾ cup salad oil
              ¼ cup vinegar
              1 teaspoon sugar
              ½ teaspoon salt
              ½ teaspoon paprika
              ½ teaspoon dry mustard
              ¼ teaspoon Tabasco sauce
              Salad greens for garnish
              Onion rings for garnish

Combine corn, celery, tomatoes, green pepper, and dill in a large bowl. Blend Avery Island Dressing ingredients together with an eggbeater. Pour dressing over vegetables in bowl. Let marinate about 1 hour before serving. Place in a serving bowl lined with salad greens. Garnish with onion rings.

Serves: 6.

Bloody Mary Mix Aspic

2 envelopes unflavored gelatin
2 cups Tabasco Bloody Mary Mix
1 bay leaf
1½ cups water
1 teaspoon salt
¼ teaspoon sugar

In a medium saucepan, sprinkle gelatin over Bloody Mary Mix. Add bay leaf. Cook over low heat, stirring constantly until gelatin dissolves, about 5 minutes. Remove from heat; remove bay leaf. Stir in remaining ingredients. Pour into 4-cup mold. Chill until firm. To serve, unmold onto serving platter. Serve with cottage cheese, seafood salad, or chicken salad.
Serves: 4.

Molded Avocado Salad

3-ounce package lemon gelatin
1 cup boiling water
1 cup mayonnaise
1 cup sour cream
1½ cups mashed avocado
3 tablespoons lemon juice
6 sprigs of parsley

In a small bowl, combine lemon gelatin and boiling water, stirring until dissolved. Cool. Combine mayonnaise, sour cream, avocado, and lemon juice in a separate bowl. Blend mayonnaise mixture and gelatin until smooth. Pour into an oiled mold and chill until firm. Garnish with sprigs of parsley.
Serves: 4.

Tomato Surprise

1 pint cherry tomatoes
½ pound bacon, cooked and crumbled
¼ teaspoon Tabasco sauce

Cut out small hole in the top of each tomato. Combine crumbled bacon with Tabasco. Spoon bacon mixture into tomatoes. Serve with food picks.
Yield: About 24 tomatoes.

Chicken and Avocado Salad

4 cups chicken, cooked and diced
½ cup chopped celery
½ cup black olives, pitted and sliced
½ cup green olives, pitted and sliced
½ cup mayonnaise
2 drops Tabasco sauce
1 large avocado, peeled and sliced
1 tablespoon lemon juice
½ teaspoon salt
¼ teaspoon pepper
6 large lettuce leaves

Blend chicken, celery, olives, mayonnaise, and Tabasco sauce. Place avocado on a dish and drizzle with lemon juice, salt, and pepper. Toss avocado lightly with chicken mixture and spoon onto lettuce leaves. Garnish with a thin slice of avocado.
Serves: 4 to 6.

Coleslaw

1 large head cabbage, shredded
1 tablespoon salt
½ green pepper, seeded and chopped
½ pimento, seeded and chopped
1 egg yolk
1 cup oil
½ teaspoon dry mustard
2 drops Tabasco sauce
½ teaspoon paprika
1 teaspoon celery salt

Place cabbage in a large bowl and sprinkle with salt. Allow to wilt for 1 hour. Drain well. Combine peppers with cabbage and toss well. In a small bowl, combine remaining ingredients and whip until thickened. Pour liquid over cabbage-pepper mixture and toss until well blended.
Serves: 6.

Texas-Style Coleslaw

1 large cabbage, shredded
1 cup sugar
1 large onion, sliced very thin
1 cup vinegar
⅔ cup corn oil
2 teaspoons dry mustard
2 teaspoons celery seed
1 teaspoon celery salt
½ teaspoon caraway seed

Place shredded cabbage in a large saucepan and cover with sugar, onion slices, vinegar, oil, dry mustard, celery seed and salt, and caraway seed. Toss well. Cover, bring to a boil, uncover, stir well, recover. Simmer 3 to 5 minutes. Cool then refrigerate for 6 hours before serving. Toss several times while being refrigerated.
Serves: 4 to 6.

Sauces and Dressings

Cerveza Salad Dressing

10½-ounce can tomato soup
¾ cup oil
½ cup *cerveza* (Mexican beer)
¼ teaspoon dry mustard
1 teaspoon salt
1 teaspoon sugar
2 teaspoons horseradish sauce
1 teaspoon Worcestershire sauce
½ small onion, minced
½ teaspoon garlic, minced
½ teaspoon pepper
2 drops Tabasco sauce

Combine all ingredients in a quart jar and shake vigorously. For a better flavor, refrigerate several days before using.
Yield: 3½ cups.

Chiled Sour Cream

Spoon this excellent sour cream-chile sauce into your baked potatoes next time instead of sour cream with chives!

7-ounce can green chiles, chopped and drained
¼ teaspoon Tabasco sauce
½ teaspoon salt
½ teaspoon paprika
1 teaspoon instant minced onions
16-ounce container sour cream

Combine green chiles, Tabasco sauce, salt, paprika, and instant minced onions in a small bowl. Let stand 30 minutes to rehydrate onions. Mix well to blend. Fold into sour cream; refrigerate 2 hours before serving.
Yield: About 3 cups.

Sour Cream Topping

A tangy baked potato topping, especially good when served at a chili party.

1½-ounce package sour cream sauce mix*
¼ cup evaporated milk
¼ cup cold water
¼ teaspoon Tabasco sauce

In mixing bowl, combine all ingredients.
Yield: topping for 6 baked potatoes.

*Or simply blend ¼ teaspoon Tabasco sauce with 6 ounces of sour cream.

Butter Sauce
(For Vegetables)

½ cup butter
½ teaspoon Tabasco sauce
1 tablespoon minced parsley or
  ½ teaspoon dried oregano

Melt butter in small saucepan. Stir in Tabasco and parsley or oregano. Brush on vegetables during grilling. *Yield: ½ cup*—enough for 1 medium-sized eggplant, 2 tomatoes, and 4 small-sized zucchini.

Three-Bean Relish

16-ounce can northern beans, plus liquid
16-ounce can pinto beans, drained
16-ounce can kidney beans, drained
2 tablespoons sugar
1 teaspoon coriander
2 teaspoons salt
¼ cup minced celery
7-ounce can green chiles
¾ cup minced onions
1 teaspoon pepper
¼ cup wine vinegar

Combine all ingredients and refrigerate for several days, stirring occasionally to blend flavors thoroughly. *Serves: 6 to 8.*

Mexican Salad Dressing

¼ teaspoon pepper
½ teaspoon chili powder
¼ teaspoon paprika
½ teaspoon dry mustard
¼ teaspoon garlic powder
½ teaspoon onion powder
½ teaspoon salt
⅓ cup vinegar
⅔ cup oil

Place all ingredients in a quart jar and shake vigorously. Store several days unrefrigerated before using. Shake frequently during this time.
Yield: 1¼ cups.

Avocado Dressing

2 large avocados, peeled and pitted
3 tablespoons lemon juice
16-ounce container sour cream
1 large clove garlic, crushed for juice only
1 teaspoon salt
4 drops Tabasco sauce

Dice avocados and place in a large bowl; sprinkle with lemon juice. Let stand 10 minutes. Puree avocados with a fork and press through a sieve. Add remaining ingredients; blend thoroughly. Cover bowl tightly and chill 2 hours before serving.
Yield: 4 cups.

Dips

===

Pickled Hot Jalapeño Dip

11½-ounce jar jalapeño pepper strips
16-ounce container sour cream
½ teaspoon salt
½ teaspoon paprika
½ teaspoon cumin powder
2 8-ounce packages cream cheese, softened
Fresh parsley for garnish
Paprika
1 large bag Frito Lay Corn Chips

Drain jalapeño pepper strips and chop well. Combine sour cream, salt, paprika, and cumin with jalapeños in a large bowl. Add cream cheese to sour cream mixture and blend until smooth. Pour into a decorative bowl and chill before serving. Garnish with fresh parsley sprigs and jalapeños, and sprinkle with paprika. Serve with corn chips.

Yield: About 5 cups.

===

Creamy Guacamole

2 ripe avocados, peeled and pureed
2 tablespoons mayonnaise
2 drops Tabasco sauce
1 tablespoon fresh lime juice
½ teaspoon Worcestershire sauce
¼ teaspoon garlic powder
½ teaspoon seasoning salt
1 teaspoon chili powder

Work avocados through a sieve or puree in a blender. Add remaining ingredients and blend until smooth. Chill until ready to serve with tortilla chips, as a salad, or with Nachos (see page 192).
Yield: About 3 cups.

Chiles and Dried Beef Dip

3 tablespoons butter
4-ounce can green chiles, chopped
4-ounce jar dried beef, diced
1 medium-sized onion, minced
1 clove garlic, minced
8 ounces cream cheese, creamed
2 tablespoons milk
4 drops Tabasco sauce

Melt butter in a heavy skillet and add green chiles, dried beef, onion, and garlic; sauté until onion is tender. In a mixing bowl, combine cream cheese and milk; blend until smooth. Add Tabasco and blend again. Chill 2 hours or until firm. Serve with crackers or chips.
Yield: 2½ cups dip.

Sombrero Chili Dip

Serve hot with corn chips for dipping.

1 pound ground beef
¼ cup minced onion
1 clove garlic, minced
8-ounce can tomato sauce
7-ounce can Ortega brand diced green chiles
16-ounce can kidney beans, drained and mashed
1 teaspoon salt

Garnish:

½ cup grated Longhorn cheese
¼ cup ripe olives, pitted and sliced
¼ cup chopped onion

Brown beef in a large skillet until crumbled. Drain. Add onion and garlic, and sauté until onion is tender. Mix in tomato sauce, chiles, beans, and salt. Heat thoroughly. Place in a chafing dish. Top with garnishes attractively arranged over meat mixture.

Serves: 6 to 8.

Mexican Hot Bean Dip

8 strips of bacon, fried and crumbled (reserve drippings)
2 16-ounce cans refried beans
1 large onion, minced
1 clove garlic, minced
2 tablespoons Tabasco sauce
2 to 3 tablespoons sour cream
Whole, pickled jalapeño peppers for garnish

Place crumbled bacon in a 2-quart saucepan with refried beans and stir well. Sauté onions and garlic in bacon drippings until tender. Add to bean mixture. Add Tabasco sauce and sour cream and blend until smooth. Chill for 1 hour. Shape into a ball and place on wax paper and chill for 1 hour. Garnish with whole, pickled jalapeño peppers.
Yield: About 4 cups.

Cottage Cheese and Green Chile Dip

A refreshing dip for vegetables or chips.

16-ounce container cottage cheese, small curd
16-ounce container sour cream
1 teaspoon salt
7-ounce can green chiles, drained
⅓ cup minced cucumbers
⅓ cup minced green onions
1 large pimento, minced
½ teaspoon Tabasco sauce

Combine all ingredients and blend until creamy. Chill 2 hours before serving.
Yield: About 4½ cups.

Mex or Tex-Mex?

Most Mexicans are as vehement in their denial of ever having had a thing to do with the creation of *chile con carne* as Texans are zealous in claiming it was created on *their* side of the Rio Grande. The latter school is undoubtedly right, but there are certainly many Mexican concoctions that have a resemblance to chili. There is one school of cooking that has developed over the years that combines the cooking of both sides of the Great River. It is called Tex-Mex and many of the dishes that have come to be considered Mexican are actually ones that were created by Mexicans *north* of the Border. Recipes in this section fall into either category, but each recipe, in its own peculiar way, goes with chili.

Chorizo with Eggs and Chile

2 chorizo (Spanish sausage)
1 tablespoon chopped onions
2 eggs, lightly beaten
¼ cup green chile sauce

Mash and heat chorizo in a well-greased heavy skillet. Add onion and mix. Turn heat low and add lightly beaten eggs and chile sauce. Stir eggs from bottom of skillet as they become firm. Cook to desired firmness. Serve at once with toast.
Serves: 1.

Easy Egg-Batter Chiles Rellenos

7-ounce can Ortega brand whole green chiles
8-ounce package Monterey Jack cheese or
  Muenster cheese
½ cup flour, seasoned with salt and pepper
3 eggs, separated
3 tablespoons flour
Oil for frying
7-ounce can Ortega brand green chile salsa

Drain and slit each chile lengthwise, just enough to remove seeds if desired. Cut cheese into strips ½-inch thick and long enough to fit into chiles. Stuff each chile with a piece of cheese. Dredge stuffed chiles in seasoned flour; set aside. Beat egg whites until stiff peaks form. Beat egg yolks until creamy. Fold yolks into whites, adding 3 tablespoons flour as you fold. Dip each stuffed chile into this egg batter and set on a small dish. Slide coated chile from dish into deep hot oil to fry (about 400° F). Fry until golden brown, about 2 minutes, turning once gently. Drain chiles on paper towels. Serve with heated green chile salsa. Leftover Chiles Rellenos are equally as good when cold.
Yield: 6 Chiles Rellenos.
Serves: 3.

Red Enchiladas

12 corn tortillas
Oil
Red chile sauce
2 cups shredded Colby cheese
1 small onion, chopped fine
4 fried eggs
Lettuce
Tomato, sliced or chopped

In a heavy skillet, fry tortillas one at a time in about an inch of oil until soft. Drain on paper towels. Heat red chile sauce; dip fried corn tortillas in sauce. Arrange on a hot serving plate in layers with cheese and onion. Use three tortillas to a serving. Fry egg and put on top. Put lettuce and tomato around plate.
Serves: 4.

Chile Con Queso

Chili with cheese, perfect over Chiles Rellenos.

4-ounce can Ortega brand diced green chiles
1 pound pasteurized processed cheese spread or American cheese, cubed
16-ounce can tomatoes, finely chopped
1 tablespoon dried minced onion
Corn chips

Heat all ingredients, except corn chips, together in a chafing dish, fondue pot, or saucepan over low heat until cheese is melted. Serve with corn chips.
Serves: 12.

Mexicana Lamb

4 cloves garlic, minced
2 teaspoons oregano
2 7-ounce cans Ortega brand green chile salsa
Salt and pepper
2 tablespoons red wine vinegar
3 tablespoons oil
4 to 5 pounds lamb, cut into 1½-inch cubes

Combine all ingredients, except lamb. Pour mixture over lamb cubes in a glass or enamel dish and mix thoroughly. Cover and let stand overnight in refrigerator. Place lamb cubes on skewers and barbecue, basting with remaining marinade.
Serves: 6.

Chorizo with Green Peppers

1½ pounds chorizo, chopped
2 medium-sized onions, sliced
2 green peppers, seeded and sliced
2 tablespoons jalapeño peppers, chopped
1 teaspoon lemon juice
1 tablespoon coriander
½ teaspoon Mexican oregano*

Lightly brown chorizo in a heavy skillet. Add remaining ingredients, stirring to blend. Reduce heat to simmer, cover, and cook for 20 to 25 minutes or until peppers are tender but still slightly firm.
Serves: 4.

*Available in epicurean shops.

Beef Tamales

Filling:

1 pound cubed beef
3 tablespoons oil
1 teaspoon minced garlic
½ teaspoon salt
2 tablespoons cornstarch
½ teaspoon oregano, crumbled
1 cup Red Chile Sauce (see page 195)
15½-ounce can beef stock

Husks and Cornmeal Wrap:

2 cups masa flour
1 teaspoon salt
¾ cup lard
1 cup warm water
36 corn husks, trimmed
(available in epicurean shops)

Brown beef lightly in oil with garlic. When browned on all sides, cover with water and reduce heat to simmer for 1½ hours or until beef pulls apart easily. In a small bowl, combine salt, cornstarch, oregano, and red chile sauce with beef stock until cornstarch dissolves. Add to beef and stir until thickened. If too thin, cook a little longer with the lid off until mixture thickens.

To prepare casing for tamales:
Combine masa flour and salt in a small bowl. Slowly add masa flour to softened lard and beat until light and fluffy. Soak the husks in water to soften. Rinse well. Open husks and spread center portion with a small amount of masa mixture (this will be the coating around the beef mixture), allowing a 2-inch edge. Spoon a small

amount of thickened beef mixture on to center of masa spread. Fold one side of husk over mixture. This will cover the filling with the masa. Roll the husk and fold over the ends.

To heat, place tamales in a shallow saucepan with a little water, cover, and steam 15 minutes over a low flame.

Yield: 36 tamales (10 to 12 servings).

Burritos

1 pound ground beef
1 large onion, chopped
1 clove garlic, chopped
7-ounce can Ortega brand green chile salsa
4-ounce can Ortega brand diced green chiles
2 cups grated Monterey Jack cheese
Bread crumbs
12 flour tortillas
Water
Oil for frying

Brown beef in a heavy skillet until crumbly. Drain. Add onion and garlic and cook until wilted. Remove skillet from heat and stir in salsa, chiles, and cheese. Stir in enough bread crumbs to thicken mixture (about 2 tablespoons). Cool. Place $1/12$ of meat mixture in center of each tortilla. Brush edges of tortilla lightly with water. Fold one side of tortilla over filling, then fold over other side. Fold ends over the same way to form a 4-inch square burrito. Drop immediately into deep fat heated to 380° F. Fry 5 minutes, turning burritos to brown on all sides. Drain on absorbent paper and serve at once. These are also delicious served cold.

Yield: 12 burritos. Serves: 4.

Huevos Rancheros

½ pound beef roast, cut into 2-inch strips
2 tablespoons oil
Water
8 green chiles, blanched and seeded
8 corn tortillas
Oil for frying
8 eggs
4 tablespoons butter
2 cups Queso Blanco (white cheese) or mozzarella

Brown beef in oil, cover with water, and cook until meat pulls apart in strings (about 1½ hours). It may be necessary to add more water to prevent sticking. Set aside. Chop green chiles and add to stringy beef; cover and remove from heat. In a separate skillet, fry tortillas in oil until soft; remove and keep warm. Fry eggs in butter until soft and set aside. Place one egg on a tortilla and spread a small portion of beef mixture over egg. Roll and place on a cookie sheet. Repeat until all tortillas are filled. Sprinkle with cheese and place under a broiler until cheese bubbles. Serve with refried beans and a salad.
Serves: 4.

Nachos

For those who prefer them hotter, add diced green chiles to bean-salsa mixture.

4 corn tortillas
Oil or lard
½ cup refried beans

¼ cup Ortega brand green chile salsa
2 cups grated Monterey Jack cheese

Fry tortillas until crisp in shallow oil. Drain and let stand at room temperature. Combine beans and salsa and heat until bubbly. Just before serving, spread beans over tortillas to within ½ inch of the edge. Sprinkle cheese over bean mixture and broil until cheese melts and is bubbly. Cut each tortilla into 6 to 8 wedges and serve immediately.
Serves: 4 to 6.

Breakfast Tacos

3 tablespoons oil
3 medium-sized potatoes, shredded
2 green onions, chopped
1½ teaspoon salt
8 flour tortillas
6 eggs, beaten
½ pound hot sausage, fried, crumbled, and drained
1 cup jalapeño pepper sauce

Heat oil in a large skillet and fry shredded potatoes with the onions until both are tender. Add salt, stirring until blended. Preheat oven to 350° F; heat tortillas for 15 minutes in a pie tin that has been covered with aluminum foil. While the tortillas are heating, fry the eggs and set aside. Combine potatoes, eggs, and sausage; toss gently. Remove tortillas from oven and fill each tortilla evenly with egg mixture. Serve very hot. Jalapeño sauce is to be served on the side for those who wish to use it.
Yield: 8 tacos. Serves: 3 to 4.

La Carne Hacienda

2 pounds lean stew beef or pork shoulder, cut into 1-inch
  cubes
3 tablespoons flour
1 teaspoon salt
½ teaspoon pepper
2 tablespoons lard or oil
2 large cloves garlic, minced
2 large onions, chopped
1 cup water
2 7-ounce cans Ortega brand green chile salsa
¼ teaspoon ground cloves
½ teaspoon cinnamon
3 tablespoons blanched slivered almonds
¼ cup raisins
2 4-ounce cans Ortega brand sliced green chiles
1 cup raw rice, cooked to package directions

In plastic bag, shake meat with flour, salt, and pepper.
Brown meat with lard in a large skillet. Add garlic,
onion, water, and salsa. Simmer, covered, 1 hour or until
meat is tender. Add remaining ingredients, except rice,
and stir. Simmer, covered, 15 minutes. Serve over rice.
Serves: 6.

Tacos

12 corn tortillas
Oil or lard for frying
1½ pounds chorizo (or ground beef), fried and chopped
2 cups shredded lettuce
2 cups shredded Cheddar cheese

2 tomatoes, diced
7-ounce can Ortega brand taco sauce or green chile salsa

Fry one tortilla at a time in about ½ inch of hot oil over medium heat until tortilla becomes soft (just a few seconds). Fold in half and hold slightly open with tongs or two forks so there will be a space between the folded tortilla for filling to be added later. Fry the tortilla until crisp and light brown, turning as necessary. Fill tacos with chorizo, lettuce, cheese, tomatoes, and taco sauce to taste.
Yield: 12 tacos. Serves: 3 to 4.

Red Chile Sauce

SALSA ROJO

2 cups red chiles (about 40 to 50 chiles)
2 small onions, chopped
1 clove garlic, minced
2 tablespoons oil
1 cup chicken broth
1 teaspoon cumin powder
2 teaspoons salt
1 teaspoon oregano

Remove seeds and veins from chiles and put in a medium saucepan; add onions, garlic, and oil. Heat until steaming; cover and simmer about 15 minutes at very low heat. Stir frequently to avoid sticking. Add remaining ingredients; blend well. Continue cooking at very low heat for 60 minutes or until sauce thickens. Stir occasionally.
Yield: 3 cups.

Green Chile Sauce

SALSA VERDE

2 7-ounce cans green chiles
2 large tomatoes, peeled and minced
2 jalapeño peppers, minced
½ teaspoon sugar
1 teaspoon salt
½ teaspoon pepper
1 large onion, minced
1 clove garlic, minced
¼ cup oil

Combine all ingredients, except oil, in a saucepan. Boil chile mixture for 1 minute, cover, and remove from heat. Cool. Stir in oil and let stand 1 hour more.
Yield: 3 cups.

Mustard-Chili Salsa

1 cup minced onions
2 cloves garlic, minced
½ cup (1 stick) butter
½ cup green chile salsa
1 teaspoon dry mustard
1 teaspoon prepared mustard
1 teaspoon salt
¼ cup minced pimentos

Sauté onion and garlic in butter until onions are transparent. Simmer about 10 minutes. Add remaining ingredients, blend well, cover, and simmer 10 minutes. Cook.

Pour into a bowl and refrigerate overnight for an excellent marinade sauce.
Yield: 2½ cups.

Green Enchiladas

4 tablespoons oil
3 medium-sized onions, chopped
16-ounce can tomatoes, drained and chopped
3 7-ounce cans green chiles, chopped
1½ cups heavy cream
18 to 20 tortillas
3 cups grated sharp cheese
3 cups shredded lettuce

Heat oil in a saucepan and sauté onions until tender. Add tomatoes and chiles; stir until heated. Slowly add cream, stirring until well blended. Simmer, uncovered, until mixture is slightly thickened, about 30 minutes. Fry tortillas 30 seconds on each side in ½ inch of fat in a heavy skillet. Place tortilla on a plate. Top with sauce and then cheese. Add another tortilla and repeat two more times. A stack of three is a serving. Garnish with shredded lettuce for added flavor and color. Salt to taste.
Yield: 18 to 20 enchiladas. Serves: 6 to 8.

Mexican-Style Spoon Bread

3 eggs, beaten
1¼ teaspoons baking powder
1 teaspoon salt
½ teaspoon soda
¾ cup buttermilk

½ teaspoon sugar
16-ounce can cream-style corn
4-ounce can chiles, chopped
1⅔ cup grated Parmesan cheese

Combine all ingredients, except chiles and Parmesan cheese, and mix well. Pour half of the batter into a greased 8-by-8-inch baking dish. Sprinkle with half the chiles and half the cheese, pour remaining batter and top with chiles and cheese. Preheat oven to 375° F for 10 minutes. Bake spoon bread for 60 minutes. Cool and serve.
Serves: 6.

Eggnog

ROMPOPE

The Texas Mexicans serve this drink, which is similar to our Christmas eggnog. Top with a sprinkle of cinnamon.

2 quarts milk
3 cups sugar
3 teaspoons vanilla
1½ dozen eggs, lightly beaten
1 pint Mexican liqueur or 1 pint bourbon
1 teaspoon rum flavoring

Combine milk and sugar in a large saucepan; stir until sugar is dissolved. Add vanilla and scald. Remove immediately from heat and cool to lukewarm. Slowly add beaten eggs, stirring continuously to blend well. Return to heat to thicken slightly but do not boil. Remove from heat and add liqueur and rum flavoring. Serve chilled in glasses.
Yield: About 3 quarts.

Mexican Chocolate Drink

Mexican chocolate is very similar to our sweet chocolate used in candy bars. If using sweet chocolate, add a pinch of cinnamon and ginger to the mixture for that Mexican taste.

> 12 squares (12 oz.) Mexican chocolate
> 2 quarts milk
> 2 tablespoons sugar
> 1 teaspoon vanilla (optional)
> 4 egg yolks, beaten

Grate chocolate into a 3-quart saucepan. Add about 2 cups milk to chocolate; cook on very low heat until chocolate dissolves. Add remaining milk. Add sugar and vanilla; stir until sugar dissolves. Slowly add beaten egg yolks to milk, stirring continuously until well blended. Remove from heat and stir until froth disappears. Serve chilled or heated.
Yield: 2½ quarts.

Sopaipillas

Can be served as bread, with honey as dessert, or stuffed as a main dish.

> 1 package activated dry yeast
> ¼ cup water
> 1 cup milk
> 2 tablespoons shortening
> 1 teaspoon salt

2 teaspoons sugar
3 cups flour
1 teaspoon baking powder
Vegetable oil for deep frying

Dissolve yeast in warm water. Scald milk; add shortening, salt, sugar, and allow to cool to lukewarm. Add yeast to milk mixture. Sift flour and baking powder together into a large mixing bowl, making a well in the center. Pour liquid ingredients into the well and work into a dough. Knead until smooth and elastic, about 15 minutes. Cover with wax paper or plastic wrap and set aside for 20 minutes. Roll dough out to about ¼-inch thickness and cut into triangles or squares, about 3 inches across. Fry in hot oil (about 425° F) until golden on each side.
Yield: About 36 puffs.

Gazpacho

10-ounce can Snap-E-Tom brand tomato cocktail
½ medium-sized cucumber, cut up
1 medium-sized tomato, cut up
1 tablespoon sugar
¼ cup red wine vinegar
¼ cup salad oil
2 10-ounce cans Snap-E-Tom brand tomato cocktail
1 medium-sized tomato, finely chopped
½ medium-sized cucumber, finely chopped
1 onion, finely chopped

Blend together in a blender the first six ingredients. Add remaining 2 cans tomato cocktail, finely chopped tomato, cucumber, and onion. Serve very cold with at least two of the following garnishes: croutons, chopped hard-boiled egg whites, chopped green peppers, chopped fresh onion.
Serves: 6.

Mexican Pea Soup

This old recipe is excellent served with Mexican-Style Spoon Bread (see page 197).

16-ounce package dry peas
1 quart water
1 cup chopped celery
1 large onion, chopped
1 carrot, thinly sliced
3 medium-sized potatoes, diced
1 ham bone
3 cups diced ham
½ cup ham fat
½ teaspoon ginger
Salt to taste
½ teaspoon pepper

Wash peas thoroughly, cover with water, and allow to soak overnight. Add remaining ingredients and simmer, covered, stirring occasionally, 2½ hours.
Serves: 6.

Empanadas

A Mexican meat pie.

1¼ cups instant minced onion
1¼ cups water
⅔ cup olive or salad oil
5 pounds ground beef
½ can (gallon) No. 10 tomatoes, broken up
1¼ cups raisins or currants

1¼ cups green olives, pitted and chopped
⅔ cup chili powder
3 tablespoons salt
2½ tablespoons paprika
2 tablespoons oregano leaves, crushed
15 hard-boiled eggs, chopped
7½ pounds pie dough

Combine onion and water to rehydrate for 10 minutes; set aside. Heat oil in a large skillet until hot. Add onion and beef and brown 5 minutes. Drain excess fat. Stir in tomatoes, raisins, olives, chili powder, salt, paprika, and oregano. Cook, uncovered, for 5 minutes, stirring occasionally. Remove from heat and stir in eggs, then cool. Divide dough into 50 portions. On a lightly floured board, roll each separately into a 6-inch circle, ⅛-inch thick. Spoon about ⅓ cup meat mixture onto one side of each circle. Moisten edges with water; fold pastry over filling to form a semicircle. Press edges to seal; crimp. Prick tops of pastries to allow steam to escape. (If desired, brush tops with egg yolk beaten with water.) Place on cookie sheets. Bake in a preheated 400° F oven for 30 minutes or until golden brown. Serve hot.
Yield: 50 empanadas.

Mexican Refried Beans

1 pound pinto beans, soaked overnight
4 tablespoons bacon drippings
1 teaspoon onion juice
1½ teaspoons salt
1 teaspoon Tabasco sauce
1 teaspoon lemon juice
2 tablespoons oil

Drain soaked beans well, rinse, and recover with hot water. Add the remaining ingredients, stir well, cover, and simmer for 4 hours. Stir occasionally. Uncover and continue simmering 1 to 2 hours or until almost all the liquids are cooked away. Stir often to prevent sticking. Remove from heat and mash until smooth. Cool.

Heat oil in a heavy skillet. Add beans and heat until bubbling. Turn to brown other side, adding more oil if necessary. Spoon to serve.

Serves: 6 to 8.

Drinks–What Warms You Up; What Cools You Down

It only stands to reason: Sometimes a drink should get you "warmed up" for chili, but, most likely, the drink should either help wash it down or cool you off. Here is a passel of drinks that fit right in, one for every need.

For reasons of heritage, tequila drinks are most usually associated with chili happenings, and there are several, from Prickly Perrier to Arizona Eye-Opener. Many of the drinks have been concocted especially for this cookbook; others are traditional—the Margarita and the Tequila Sunrise, to mention a couple. But whatever the tequila drink, it will certainly enhance the flavor of chili (or tone it down). And tequila, which is made from the Mexican agave plant, is said by one distiller to "contain a high percentage of vitamins, hormones, and some enzymes. It is also used as a remedy for kidney ailments and other stomach troubles (when used in moderation)." What more could one ask?

There are beer drinks and wine drinks and Prairie Cherry (also original), and just some plain "good with anything" drinks. Cheers!

204

Red-Eye

Must have been invented just for chili.

4 ounces tomato juice, chilled
Dash Worcestershire sauce
Beer, chilled

Pour tomato juice into 12-ounce pilsner glass; add Worcestershire sauce and fill glass with beer. Repeat as long as the chili holds out.

Key Biscayne Wine Cooler

3 ounces white or rosé wine
Grapefruit soft drink
Slice of lime

Pour wine over rocks in tall cocktail glass and fill with grapefruit soft drink. Garnish with lime.

Port Isabel Wine Spritzer

4 ounces dry white wine
4 ounces Perrier water
Juice of ½ lime
Wedge of lime

Mix wine and Perrier with cracked ice in tall cocktail glass. Stir in lime juice. Rub edge of glass with wedge and place wedge in drink.

Planters' Punch

Juice of 1 lime
Juice of 1 lemon
Juice of 1 small orange
1 tablespoon powdered sugar
2 ounces Meyers's rum
Pineapple cube, cherry, and orange slice for garnish

Pour all ingredients into 16-ounce glass or mug filled with cracked ice. Stir until glass is frosty. Garnish with pineapple cube, cherry, and orange slice on long toothpick.

Sazerac Cocktail

New Orleans made many things famous. But this is the drink that made New Orleans *famous.*

½ ounce Pernod
½ lump sugar
2 dashes bitters
Water
2 ice cubes
2 ounces rye whiskey
Lemon twist for garnish

Pour Pernod into Old-Fashioned glass and swirl around until inside of glass is coated. Add sugar and bitters and enough water to cover sugar. Mix until sugar is dissolved. Add ice and whiskey; stir very well. Garnish with twist of lemon.

Pepsi Light-ning

2 ounces moonshine
Pepsi Light
Wedge of lime

In tall glass, pour moonshine over ice; fill glass with Pepsi Light and sprinkle juice of lime into mixture. Drop lime in drink and stand back.

Cuba Libre

2 ounces rum
Ice
Pepsi
Juice of ½ lime

In tall glass, pour rum over ice. Fill glass with Pepsi and squeeze lime into mixture.

Ramos Gin Fizz

Juice of ½ lemon
1 egg white
1 teaspoon confectioners' sugar
1½ ounces dry gin
2 teaspoons sweet cream
Dash orange flower water
Club soda

Shake all ingredients well, except club soda, and strain into tall cocktail glass. Fill with club soda and stir.

Nassau Bloody Mary

1½ ounces vodka
6 ounces V-8 cocktail juice
3 dashes Tabasco sauce
4 dashes Worcestershire sauce
½ teaspoon instant bouillon
Juice of ½ lime
¼ teaspoon seasoning salt
Salt and pepper to taste
Lime wedge for garnish
Stalk celery for garnish

Stir together all ingredients in mixing glass with cracked ice. Pour over rocks in tall cocktail glass and garnish with lime wedge and stalk of celery.

Sangría

Before, during, or after a chili party.

1 bottle rosé or red wine
½ cup sugar
½ cup lemon juice
1 orange, sliced
1 lemon, sliced
2 ounces Triple Sec
2 ounces brandy
8 ounces club soda

Combine all ingredients, except club soda, in pitcher. Chill for 2 hours. Add club soda immediately before serving.
Serves: 4.

Aztec Punch

For a large, friendly gathering.

> 1 gallon Montezuma tequila
> Juice of 12 lemons
> 4 16-ounce cans grapefruit juice
> 2 quarts strong tea
> 1½ teaspoons cinnamon
> 1½ ounces bitters

Add all ingredients to a large bowl. Let stand 2 hours before blending.
Yield: 124 cups.

Mint Julep

> 1 teaspoon powdered sugar
> 2 teaspoons water
> Shaved ice
> 3 ounces Rebel Yell bourbon
> 3 sprigs fresh mint

In Old-Fashioned glass (silver mug if proper etiquette is desired), dissolve sugar in water. In separate glass, muddle leaves stripped from one sprig of mint in bourbon, until strong mint aroma is detected. Strain bourbon through fine sieve or cheesecloth into sugar-water mixture and ice. Stir until glass is frosted, being careful not to melt frost with fingers. Stick remaining two sprigs of mint into side of glass and sprinkle with powdered sugar. Serve respectfully.

Tennessee Tonic

2 ounces Jack Daniels Black Label whiskey
Lump sugar
Cracked ice
Branch water*

Pour Jack Daniels over sugar in Old-Fashioned glass and muddle until sugar is dissolved. Fill glass with cracked ice and add splash of water.

*Any nonchlorinated water, preferably from south of the Mason-Dixon line.

Prickly Perrier

2 ounces tequila
Perrier water
Wedge lime

Pour tequila over rocks in Old-Fashioned glass. Add Perrier, stir, and add lime.

Prairie Cherry

1½ ounces gin
Juice of ½ lime
2 ounces maraschino cherry juice
Ice cubes
Quinine water

In tall cocktail glass, mix all ingredients, except quinine (tonic). Stir, add ice cubes, and fill with quinine water.

Arizona Eye-Opener

2 ounces vodka
1 ounce tequila
½ ounce Triple Sec
4 ounces orange juice

Mix together with ice and pour entire mixture into tall cocktail glass.

Nashville Eggnog

Serves 12, or 9, or 6—depending upon size of fire that needs to be put out.

2 quarts prepared eggnog
12 ounces Jack Daniels whiskey
6 ounces brandy
Nutmeg

Mix eggnog, whiskey, and brandy in punch bowl. Sprinkle with nutmeg and chill for 2 hours.

Mexican Martini

2 ounces tequila
½ ounce dry vermouth
Dash vanilla extract

Mix tequila, vermouth, and vanilla extract with ice; strain into stemmed Martini glass.

Salty Dog

2 ounces dry gin*
2 ounces grapefruit juice
Juice of ½ lime
¼ teaspoon salt

Mix all ingredients in drink-mixing glass and strain into Whiskey Sour glass.

*For Prairie Dog, substitute 2 ounces tequila.

Tequila Tropical

1½ Montezuma tequila
½ ounce grenadine
3 ounces orange juice
1 teaspoon lemon juice
Orange slice and cherry for garnish

Pour all ingredients into highball glass over cracked ice. Garnish with orange slice and cherry.

Tequila Ghost

2 parts Montezuma tequila
1 part Pernod
½ part fresh lemon juice

Mix all ingredients together and shake well with cracked ice. Strain into cocktail glass.

Golden Knife

2 ounces Gold Montezuma tequila
1½ ounces lemon juice
2 teaspoons sugar
2 dashes bitters
1 small egg
Iced club soda
Salt

Blend tequila, lemon juice, sugar, bitters, and egg with ice. Strain into 14-ounce glass with ice. Fill with club soda. Sprinkle with salt.

Tequila Buttermilk

1½ ounces Montezuma tequila
1 bottle lemon/lime soft drink
Cracked ice

Put ingredients in blender and mix; garnish with lemon or lime wedge.

Tequila Manhattan

2 ounces tequila
1 ounce sweet vermouth
Wedge of lime

Serve on rocks in Old-Fashioned glass. Garnish with cherry and orange slice on toothpick.

Tequila Stinger

1½ ounces tequila
1 ounce green crème de menthe

Stir tequila and crème de menthe with cracked ice; strain and serve in stemmed cocktail glass, or serve on the rocks.

Cuervo Fresa

1½ ounces Jose Cuervo tequila
¾ ounce strawberry liqueur*
½ ounce lime juice
¼ teaspoon orange bitters
1 slice lime for garnish
1 fresh strawberry for garnish

Shake tequila, strawberry liqueur, lime juice, and bitters well with ice. Strain over rocks. Garnish with lime and strawberry.

*If strawberry liqueur is not available, use ½ cup fresh, mashed strawberries, well sugared.

Horny Bull

1 ounce Montezuma tequila
Ice
6 ounces orange juice

Pour tequila over crushed ice in unusual glassware—mason jar, beer mug, bud vase. Fill with orange juice.

Café Tequila

Crushed ice
1½ ounces Jose Cuervo tequila
1 teaspoon sugar
½ ounce lemon juice
Double-strength coffee

Fill highball glass to rim with crushed ice. Add tequila, sugar, and lemon juice. Pour coffee over ice to fill glass.

Tequila Caramba!

1½ ounces tequila
3 ounces grapefruit juice
1 tablespoon sugar
Cracked ice
Club soda

Shake all ingredients well, except club soda, with cracked ice. Add club soda; serve in highball glass.

Tequila Sour

1 teaspoon powdered sugar
Juice of ½ lemon
2½ ounces tequila
Ice
Slice of lemon for garnish

Shake ingredients well with ice and serve in 8-ounce glass. Garnish with a slice of lemon.

Tequila Piña

1½ ounces Montezuma tequila
3 ounces pineapple juice
1 ounce lime juice
Sugar to taste

Mix together all ingredients, shake, and serve on rocks in tall, frosted Collins glass.

For a refreshingly different cooler, serve on the rocks with club soda.

Tequila Honey

1½ ounce tequila
1 teaspoon honey
Juice of ½ lime
Dash of orange bitters

Combine all ingredients. Shake with ice and serve in cordial glasses.

Tequila Fizz

2 ounces tequila
Juice of ½ lime
½ teaspoon sugar
Dash orange bitters
Club soda
Wedge of lime for garnish

Mix together tequila, lime, sugar, and bitters in mixing glass. Pour over rocks in tall glass and fill with club soda. Garnish with lime wedge.

Tequila Sunrise

To get things started.

>1½ ounces tequila
>½ ounce fresh lime juice
>2 ounces orange juice
>2 dashes grenadine
>Wedge of lime for garnish

Mix tequila, lime juice, and orange juice in a tall glass. Add grenadine, allowing it to sink to bottom. Do not stir after grenadine is added. Serve over ice and garnish with lime.

Tequila Sunset

And to end the evening . . .

>1½ ounces tequila
>½ ounce lime juice
>1 ounce grenadine
>Crushed ice
>Wedge of lime

Place tequila, lime juice, grenadine, and ice into blender and blend at low speed for 10 seconds. Pour into champagne glass. Garnish with lime wedge.

Margarita

½ ounce Triple Sec
1½ ounces tequila
Crushed ice
Juice of ½ lemon or lime
Salt

Stir Triple Sec and tequila with crushed ice in a mixing glass. Rub rim of a 3-ounce glass with a lemon or lime; dip glass into salt. Strain and pour into glass.

Bloody Maria

1½ ounces tequila
6 ounces tomato juice
2 dashes Tabasco sauce
2 dashes Worcestershire sauce
Juice of ½ lime
¼ teaspoon seasoning salt
Salt and pepper to taste
Wedge of lime for garnish

Mix ingredients together in mixing glass and pour over cracked ice in tall glass. Garnish with wedge of lime.

Tequila Boilermaker

1 ounce tequila
Schooner Budweiser beer

Pour shot glass of tequila into beer.

Desserts–To Put Out the Fire

Desserts, like drinks, should probably have some sort of soothing effect, so here are some balmy "good endings" for a chili bash (or any *bash,* for that matter). There are some traditional Southwestern favorites here, including the ancient recipe for "Cactus Candy," which, after several months of research, turned up in the memory of a third-generation Mexican candy company owner in San Antonio. Most are less complicated than the Cactus Candy technique—simple, in fact. But each one was created with chili in mind.

Cactus Candy

An ancient recipe, verified by Ramsey Segovia of the Segovia Candy Co. of San Antonio. He was taught the method by his father, who, in turn, was taught by his father. Be prepared! The recipe takes about three days. But, if done right, it is worth it.*

*If you're not successful, don't despair. Apparently, it takes a few times to make it perfectly. As Mr. Segovia puts it, "You have to have delicacy to do it right."

Locate a bisnaga cactus; if you're in the Southwest, it will be easy. Soak the leaves in water for at least 24 hours. Using heavy gloves, remove the thorns with a knife. Soak the leaves in a solution of "cal" (lime) and water overnight. Use approximately 1 teaspoon of lime for each leaf. This is an important ingredient, because it causes the necessary coating to develop.

After soaking overnight, dip the leaves in a bowl of cool, clean water to remove excess lime. Remove them from the bowl and place in a pot of water. Over a low to medium-low flame, allow the water to boil slowly. When the leaves are firm, put them in another bowl of cool water, and poke each leaf a few times with a barbecue fork. After each leaf is perforated, put the whole batch in yet another kettle of cool water.

Over a low to medium-low flame, sprinkle 2 pounds of sugar for each pound of bisnaga. Let it boil slowly for about 20 to 25 minutes. Turn off the flame and allow to sit for a few minutes. Put a "blanket" of sugar over the leaves and turn the flame back on to the same heating level. Again, let it boil slowly for about 20 to 25 minutes, stirring gently (and frequently) with a slotted spoon. Turn the flame off and allow to sit a few minutes. Repeat the "sugar blanket" routine two more times (three layers in all).

By the third "blanket," the bisnaga leaves should begin to feel like chewed chewing gum. At this point, carefully drain them, and you've got cactus candy.

Ice-Cream Charlotte

3-dozen ladyfingers, split
½ gallon ice cream, softened
4 tablespoons instant coffee
2 tablespoons heavy cream
6 tablespoons rum
1 cup heavy cream, whipped
1 large Hershey bar, chilled
6 maraschino cherries, split

Line the sides and bottom of a 4-quart soufflé dish with ladyfingers. Place softened ice cream in a large bowl. In a glass, dissolve instant coffee with 2 tablespoons heavy cream; add rum, stirring to blend. Add rum mixture to softened ice cream and whip with a mixer at high speed. Add whipped cream to ice cream and blend thoroughly. Pour into bowl lined with ladyfingers. Shave curls of chocolate bar onto center and arrange a circle of cherries for decoration.
Serves: 6 to 8.

Italian Ices

Recipes yield about 1 quart of each flavor.

Lemon Ice: 2½ cups water
       1½ cups sugar
       1½ cups lemon juice

Bring water and sugar to a boil in 2-quart saucepan, stirring until sugar dissolves. Cook for 5 minutes. Remove from heat and allow to cool to room temperature. Stir in lemon juice, making sure lemon is thoroughly blended through syrup mixture. Pour into shallow aluminum tray (about 1 inch depth of mixture) and place in freezing compartment of refrigerator. Stir mixture once every 20 minutes, making sure to blend into mixture any ice particles that have formed around edges. When it forms the texture of snow, it is finished. For coarser texture, freeze this mixture again and crush with blender.

Raspberry Ice: 2½ cups water
      1½ cups sugar
      1 cup pureed raspberries

Follow exactly same directions as with lemon ice, making sure raspberry puree is thoroughly blended with syrup.

Strawberry Ice: 1½ cups water
      1 cup sugar
      2½ cups fresh or frozen strawberries,
       pureed
      Lemon juice (optional)

Follow same instructions as before. A slight amount (to taste) of lemon juice may be added to mixture when stirring in strawberry puree if tartness is desired.

Cherry Ice:

    2 cups water
    1½ cups sugar
    2 cups pitted, pureed cherries
    Lemon juice (optional)

Follow same instructions. If sour cherry ice is desired, cut sugar to 1 cup and add juice of ½ lemon.

Lemon Snowballs

    3 eggs, separated
    1 cup sugar
    2½ to 3 tablespoons water
    1 lemon rind, grated
    2½ tablespoons lemon juice
    1 cup flour
    1 teaspoon cornstarch
    2½ teaspoons baking powder
    Powdered sugar

Beat egg yolks with sugar until thickened and even colored. In a separate bowl combine water, lemon rind, and juice thoroughly. Add to egg yolks, blending thoroughly. Combine flour, cornstarch, and baking powder and add to egg yolk-lemon mixture. Beat egg whites to soft peaks. Fold egg whites into batter. Spoon into greased muffin tins, filling half full. Place muffin tins into a roasting pan filled with 2 inches of water. Cover roaster and steam muffins in a preheated 350° F oven for 30 minutes. Remove from oven and dust heavily with powdered sugar.

Yield: 12 lemon snowballs.

Orange Sherbet

1 cup sugar
2 cups milk
1 orange rind, grated
2 cups heavy cream, whipped
6 tablespoons frozen orange juice concentrate
3 egg whites
1 teaspoon cream of tartar
Mandarin orange sections for garnish

Combine sugar and milk, stirring until sugar dissolves. Slowly add grated orange rind until blended. Fold in whipped cream, stirring several times. Slowly add frozen orange juice concentrate to whipped cream mixture. In a separate bowl whip egg whites and cream of tartar until egg whites form soft peaks. Fold egg whites into whipped cream mixture until uniform in color. Pour into ice cube trays and chill for 1½ hours. To serve, scoop out sherbet and garnish with mandarin orange sections.
Serves: 6.

Harry Carey, Jr.'s Chocolate Mousse

1½ cups hot milk
12-ounce package chocolate bits
2 eggs
2 tablespoons sugar
1 teaspoon vanilla

Heat milk to hot but not boiling. Place bits in a blender. Pour hot milk on whirling bits (be careful of the splashing). Add whole eggs, sugar, and vanilla. Blend a few seconds. Pour into small cups or dessert dishes. Chill.
Serves: 8 to 10.

Frozen Orange Prune Cream

¼ cup sugar
2 eggs, beaten lightly
½ cup honey
2 cups (1 pint) heavy cream
6 tablespoons frozen concentrated orange juice
1 25-ounce jar cooked prunes, pitted and chopped

Gradually beat eggs into sugar, one at a time. Slowly add honey, cream, and orange juice. Beat until thickened. Freeze until half frozen. Beat again, until smooth and fluffy. Fold in prunes. Place in covered container and freeze until hard. Garnish with prunes stuffed with whole blanched almonds.
Serves: 6.

Mexican Chocolate Pudding

17½-ounce package frozen dark chocolate pudding, thawed
1 teaspoon grated orange rind
½ teaspoon ground cinnamon
1 cup (half pint) heavy cream, whipped
Semisweet chocolate for garnish
Toasted almonds for garnish

Combine pudding, orange rind, and cinnamon. Stir until well blended. Chill. Serve in sherbet glasses topped with whipped cream. If desired, garnish with shaved semisweet chocolate and top with toasted almonds.
Serves: 6 to 8.

Bananas with Rum

1 cup (half pint) heavy cream
¼ cup confectioners' sugar
¼ cup dark rum
1 teaspoon vanilla
4 large bananas
¼ cup butter or margarine
¼ cup granulated sugar
Ground cloves
Toasted coconut

Beat cream and confectioners' sugar until very thick. Fold in rum and vanilla. Cut bananas into halves lengthwise. Melt butter in a heavy skillet, add sugar, and sauté bananas until golden. Place bananas on warm serving dishes and sprinkle lightly with ground cloves and toasted coconut.
Serves: 4.

Fig Puffs

An after-chili treat, to be served with generous scoops of ice cream.

1½ cups flour
1 tablespoon baking powder
¼ teaspoon salt
3 tablespoons lard
1 egg, beaten
1½ cups cream
1 cup chopped figs

Combine flour, baking powder, and salt in a mixing bowl. Add lard and mash with a fork until crumbly. Add

egg and cream and beat to a thick batter. Fold in figs. Spoon into greased muffin tins, filling half full. Bake in a preheated 350° F oven for 20 to 25 minutes.
Yield: 12 fig puffs.

Brandied Fruit

28-ounce can pineapple chunks
10-ounce jar maraschino cherries
3 oranges, peeled and sectioned
6 figs, cut in half
28-ounce can apricots, drained
2 cups brandy
¼ cup sugar

Combine all ingredients in a covered jar and let stand unrefrigerated for 3 days to marinate fruit. Serve topped with whipped cream.
Serves: 4 to 6.

Coconut Squares

1 cup butter
2 cups flour
1 tablespoon baking powder
1 teaspoon salt
3 eggs
2 teaspoons vanilla
2 cups coconut

Melt butter and add remaining ingredients and blend thoroughly. Pour into a well-greased 9-by-13-inch baking dish and bake at 350° F for 45 to 50 minutes, or until coconut is slightly browned. Cut into squares when cooled.
Yield: 24 squares.

Bread Pudding

6 cups diced white bread
½ cup butter or margarine, melted
1 teaspoon ground cinnamon
½ teaspoon ground cloves
½ cup sugar
1 pound 6-ounce can sliced apples
½ cup chopped almonds
1 cup grated sharp Cheddar cheese
2 cups port wine, heated to steaming

In a large skillet, sauté bread in butter over medium heat until golden brown. Remove from heat; add spices and sugar. Pour half of the mixture into a greased 9-by-5-by-3-inch loaf pan. Sprinkle with apples, almonds, and cheese. Pour remaining bread mixture over apples. Bake in a preheated 350° F oven for 30 minutes, or until top is brown and crusty. Spoon warm into serving dishes and top with hot port wine.
Serves: 6.

Arkansas Molasses Cookies

2½ cups flour
1 teaspoon baking soda
2 teaspoons ground cinnamon
1 teaspoon ground ginger
⅓ cup shortening
½ cup sugar
1 egg, beaten
½ cup dark molasses
½ cup seedless raisins
½ cup buttermilk

Combine flour, soda, cinnamon, and ginger in a large bowl. In separate bowl, cream shortening and slowly add sugar until fluffy. Add egg and beat. Add molasses and blend well. Fold in raisins and fold again. Add buttermilk and blend well. Drop by spoonfuls, about 2 inches apart, onto a greased cookie sheet. Bake in a preheated 350° F oven for 8 to 10 minutes.
Yield: 3 dozen cookies.

Pudding with Caramel Top

⅓ cup sugar
½ teaspoon salt
3 tablespoons cornstarch
2 cups milk
1 teaspoon vanilla

Caramel Topping: 1 cup sugar
½ cup water

Combine sugar, salt, and cornstarch in a saucepan. Gradually add milk, stirring and removing all lumps. Heat to boiling for 2 minutes while stirring continuously. Add vanilla and stir well. Pour into a small mold that has been rinsed in cold water. Chill until firm. Dip into hot water to unmold. Top with caramel.

Pour sugar into a small saucepan and heat. Stir without stopping until sugar turns a light brown color. Slowly add water and bring to a boil. Remove from heat when thickened. Pour over pudding and chill before serving.
Serves: 4.

Sweet Potato Pie

6 medium-sized sweet potatoes, peeled, cubed, cooked,
    and mashed
3 eggs
1 cup sugar
½ teaspoon ground ginger
1 teaspoon ground cinnamon
½ teaspoon salt
¼ teaspoon ground cloves
½ teaspoon nutmeg
1 can evaporated milk
1 unbaked 9-inch pie shell

Combine sweet potatoes with eggs and blend well. Add
remaining ingredients and blend again. Pour into an
unbaked pie shell. Bake at 400° F for 25 minutes, then
reduce heat to 375° F for 35 to 40 minutes, or until a
toothpick inserted into the center comes out clean.
Serves: 6.

Pecan Pie

2 tablespoons butter
1 cup brown sugar
3 tablespoons flour
1 cup dark corn syrup
3 eggs, beaten
¼ teaspoon salt
Pinch of baking soda
1 teaspoon vanilla
½ teaspoon pecan flavoring
1 cup pecan pieces*
1 unbaked 9-inch pie shell

Cream butter, sugar, and flour. Add syrup and eggs; beat for 5 minutes until foamy. Add remaining ingredients and fold until blended. Pour into pie shell and bake in a preheated 350° F oven for 1 hour and 10 minutes or until pie is firm.
Serves: 6.

*For extra pecan touch, spread whole pecan pieces over top before baking.
Serves: 6.

Pecan Pralines

2½ cups brown sugar
1 teaspoon baking soda
1 cup heavy cream
¼ teaspoon salt
2 cups pecan pieces
4 tablespoons butter
½ cup pecan halves

Combine brown sugar and baking soda thoroughly in a 2-quart saucepan. Add cream and salt and heat slowly until sugar is dissolved. Cook over high heat for 5 minutes or to 210° F, stirring continuously, scraping sides and bottom of pan. Add pecan pieces and butter and heat to boiling; cook 2 minutes longer, stirring frequently. Remove from heat and cool slightly, about 2 to 3 minutes. Beat until thickened and smooth. Drop by spoonfuls onto wax paper. Top with a pecan half for garnish.
Yield: About 2½ dozen pralines.

So You're Planning a Chili Party— Or Maybe a Cookoff?

If a full-fledged chili cookoff just doesn't fit into your plans, then bring the cookoff to your house or apartment with a down-home Texas-style chili party. And if you like entertaining but are lacking an original idea, a chili party should do the trick. It's easy to put together, and if all the preparations are done in the true Texas spirit of fun, you can guarantee your guests a good time.

Your "theme," of course, should be the Old West. If weather permits, plan the party as an outdoors affair; but if the weatherman doesn't cooperate or you just want to have it inside, the right decor will create the scene.

• Western-motif earthenware plates and bowls, heavy glassware, and woven baskets displayed on red-and-white-checkered tablecloths will give you that Texas-café look. If you don't have enough small tables, card tables will do nicely.

• Kerosene lanterns or candles for when the sun goes down.

• Plenty of benches around an area designated for dancing. You may even want to "corral" the area off with rope.

• Lots of Country-and-Western music or Texas ballad records, particularly Gene Autry and Roy Rogers. A jukebox stocked with appropriate music is always a hit.

• How about a bale of hay, an old saddle, wagon wheel, or other piece of Western paraphernalia? But be sure to keep the hay far from the lanterns or candles.

Finally, to complete the picture, ask the guests to wear jeans and Western shirts (cowboy boots if they have them). You may even want to purchase enough inexpensive cowboy hats for your guests. They would make great favors and would lend to the atmosphere.

When planning party logistics, the buffet is the way to go. It's casual and fun—and gives your guests freedom to choose when and what they'd like to eat. A buffet setup also allows the host or hostess a chance to mingle and relax.

There are three ways to stage your chili party. First, cook your own chili. Second, challenge a friend to a real cookoff. Or third, have guests bring their favorite chili for everyone to sample and enjoy. Or even judge. By secret ballot.

If you opt for the first one, there are plenty of recipes in this book to choose from. You can select a typical

Western recipe, an authentic "old-time" recipe, one from a celebrity, one with unusual ingredients (which, of course, are available to you), or simply any one that sounds good. Or you can pass the book around to a few friends and let each one select a recipe to prepare for the party.

Or, if all this turns you on to the point that you want your own *real* chili cookoff, you can contact the International Chili Society, Post Office Box 2966, Newport Beach, California 92663, and they will send you a complete packet of information, which includes rules for judges, cooks, and officials; suggested events; and a wealth of information on just how to stage a full-scale chili cookoff. Then you can send your champion off to California for the World Championship Chili Cookoff.

But if you are content with the simpler backyard affair, here is a suggested menu:

LBJ Chili Dip
Chili Meatballs
Chili Buffet Ring
Chili Mini-Heroes
Chili (your own selection)
Watermelon Fruit Bowl
Crackers
Extra Tabasco, onions (chopped), and green chiles (diced and whole)
Corn Chips
Pepsi
Beer
Tequila (your own selection of drinks)

We have included in this section four recipes specially compounded for large groups. The Watermelon Fruit Bowl and tequila drinks can be found elsewhere in the book, or you can choose from any of the other recipes and simply increase the servings to accommodate the number of guests expected.

LBJ Chili Dip

6 pounds lean ground beef
½ pound bacon, fried and crumbled (reserve drippings)
1 cup flour
4 cans beef consommé
6 large onions, minced
8-ounce jar chili powder
2 teaspoons cumin powder
1 tablespoon oregano
2 tablespoons salt
6 pounds sharp Cheddar cheese, cut in chunks
Taco or tortilla chips

Combine beef and bacon and brown. Blend the flour in one fourth of the bacon drippings, stirring until smooth. Slowly add the consommé, stirring until thickened. Add thickened mixture to beef and blend well. Add onions, chili powder, cumin, oregano, and salt. Stir well. Simmer, uncovered, 1½ hours or until dip consistency. Add cheese until well blended. Refrigerate for several hours before serving. Serve with taco or tortilla chips.
Serves: 100.

Chili Buffet Ring with Chili Meatballs

1½ cups instant minced onions
1½ teaspoons instant minced garlic
1½ cups water
6 tablespoons oil
7½ cups tomato juice
6 cups corn, cooked
¾ cup chili powder
2 teaspoons salt
2 tablespoons yellow cornmeal
3 cups cold water
3 cups ripe olives, coarsely chopped
1½ dozen eggs, separated
Chili Meatballs (see page 237)

Combine minced onions, garlic, and water to rehydrate vegetables. Heat oil in a large skillet and sauté vegetables for 5 minutes. Pour in tomato juice, corn, chili powder, and salt. Mix cornmeal with water and add to skillet. Cook until mixture bubbles, stirring constantly. Remove from heat and stir in olives. Beat egg yolks and add to olives. Beat egg whites until stiff but not dry. Fold into cornmeal mixture. Spoon into three well-greased 2½-quart ring molds. Place molds in pans with 1 inch of hot water. Bake in a preheated 350° F oven 35 to 40 minutes or until set. Remove from oven and let stand for 5 minutes. Loosen edges with a spatula and invert over serving plate. Fill centers with Chili Meatballs (see recipe).
Serves: 48.

Chili Meatballs

12 pounds ground beef
4½ cups bread crumbs, soft
2 cups tomato juice
6 eggs, slightly beaten
8 tablespoons chili powder
3½ tablespoons salt
¾ cup oil
1 gallon canned tomatoes, broken up
1½ cups onion flakes
¾ cup sweet pepper flakes
1 tablespoon oregano leaves
1½ teaspoons sugar
1 gallon canned kidney beans

Combine beef, bread crumbs, tomato juice, eggs, 6 tablespoons of the chili powder, and salt in a large mixing bowl. Mix well but do not overmix. Shape into 1-inch balls. Heat oil in a large skillet. Add meatballs and brown in portions. Remove meatballs and set aside. Drain oil from skillet. Stir in tomatoes, onion flakes, pepper flakes, oregano, sugar, and remaining 2 tablespoons chili powder. Boil then reduce heat, uncovered, for 15 minutes. Add kidney beans and meatballs. Cook 15 minutes longer. Spoon into center of Chili Buffet Ring (see recipe page 236).
Serves: 48.

Chili Mini-Heroes

1 cup instant minced onions
2 tablespoons instant minced garlic
1 cup water
¾ cup oil
12 pounds ground beef
No. 10 can tomatoes, crushed
½ cup chili powder
3 tablespoons salt
1 tablespoon oregano, crumbled
2 teaspoons black pepper
48 Italian bread loaves, 3 ounces each

Combine minced onion and garlic with water, let stand to rehydrate. Heat oil in a large skillet, add onions and garlic, and sauté 2 minutes. Add beef; cook and brown in portions about 5 minutes. Stir often. Remove excess fat. Transfer to large pot. Stir in tomatoes, chili powder, salt, oregano, and pepper. Boil, reduce heat, and simmer, uncovered, 20 minutes. Heat bread until hot, split in half lengthwise. Fill each loaf with hot chili mixture. If desired, top with sliced avocado and diced tomatoes and serve with bowls of sour cream, shredded lettuce, rehydrated instant minced onions, shredded Monterey Jack or Cheddar cheese.
Serves: 48.

We think you'll agree that chili is a very personal sort of relationship, whether you cook it for yourself or for a party. The imagination that goes into its planning is as important as the ingredients themselves. The inventiveness required may be what has made it "the great American dish."

Glossary

Burrito: A taco made with a wheat flour tortilla, instead of the more common corn tortilla.

Capsicum: The general name for several kinds of peppers, including the many varieties of chile peppers. Though not all capsicums are hot, the ones that are derive their pungency from the varieties of soil in which they grow—Mexican soil being among the best of environments for hot peppers. Interestingly, the burning sensation so familiar to aficionados of Mexican and Southwestern food is, in fact, a thermal reaction! Moreover, a substance derived from capsicums has traditionally been used medicinally as a gastric stimulant.

Ranging in color from bright red, green, and yellow to orange and umber brown, capsicums include sweet red peppers, paprika, chiles, and the active ingredients in cayenne and commercial blends of chili and curry powders, barbecue spice, and pickling spice.

Cerveza: "Beer" in Spanish.

Chile: The general name for several varieties of peppers, which form the base of many Mexican and Southwestern dishes (see Chapter Five). Some of the most widely used chiles are:

—*Chipotle chiles:* Long and brown, they come dried.

—*Jalapeño chiles:* Elongated, green or yellow, and hot, they are available fresh or canned.

—*Pequin chiles:* Very small, red, and quite hot, they are available canned.

—*Pimento chiles:* Also known as bell peppers, they are sweet, green or red, and are used fresh.

—*Poblano chiles:* Large, wide, green, they are used fresh.

—*Serrano chiles:* Small, green, and very hot, they are available fresh or canned.

When fresh chiles are used, they must be roasted and skinned, the veins and seeds removed to reduce bitterness, and finally the chiles soaked in water or milk. When used for sauces, they are generally toasted and ground.

The use of particular chiles in Mexican dishes is traditional, but *any* can serve in place of another and result in only slight variations of flavor. When fresh, dried, or canned chiles are not available, commercially produced chili powder is a good substitute; in general, one tablespoon of chili powder is equivalent to one whole chile.

Chile con carne: Literally, "chile with meat," this dish is not Mexican, but rather, a product of the American Southwest and Texas.

Chiles Rellenos: Literally, "stuffed peppers"; the ingredients most often include veal, pork, shrimp, nuts, guacamole, cheese or corn, garnished with spices.

Chili mix: A brand-name preparation that contains not only chili powder, but a variety of other spices and "secret ingredients," depending whose brand you use.

Chili powder: Made from a mixture of ground chiles and cumin, it is available from a number of manufacturers in any grocery store—or you can make your own. See p. 65.

Chorizo: A spicy Mexican pork sausage made from pork, garlic, onions, vinegar, and a number of spices including chili powder, paprika, cloves, and black pepper. Fresh chorizo can hang indefinitely in a cool, well-ventilated place; canned ones are available in Mexican grocery stores. If chorizos are not available, Italian sausage may be substituted, though their flavor is somewhat different.

Cilantro: Coriander, also known as Chinese parsley. Its seeds are yellowish and very small; they give food a warm to hot flavor. Commercially, cilantro is used to flavor sausages, wild game, and gin.

Comino: "Cumin" in Spanish. A member of the parsley family, it is stronger than caraway, but similar in shape, taste, and aroma. Essential to all Indian curries, it is a primary ingredient in all commercial chili and curry powders.

Enchilada: A taco (made from tortilla that has been fried in hot fat containing chiles) that is filled with meat or cheese and smothered in brown chile sauce.

Filé: From the French verb, "filer," "to run or spin out," filé is made from dried sassafras leaves. When it is added to liquids, it binds and thickens.

Hominy: "Maíz de cacahuanzincle" in Spanish, hominy is made from kernels of corn, with the hull and germ removed, which is ground to varying degrees of coarseness. It is sold canned in grocery stores.

Masa: The cornmeal flour used in tortillas. It is made by boiling hulled corn kernels with lime, rinsing and grinding them to the desired coarseness.

Mexican oregano: Also called wild marjoram or Mexican sage, it grows wild in Mexico. Pliny prescribed it for scorpion stings. It has a full, pleasantly bitter flavor, and can be used in all dishes requiring tomatoes.

Molcajete: The three-legged stone bowl with rough interior, traditionally made of basalt, which is used as a mortar for grinding chiles, masa, etc.

Mole: Pronounced "mo-lay," it is one of the most common sauces in Mexican cooking. Used as a "smother sauce," it can be red, brown, black, or green, depending on the particular ingredients; often included are: various chiles, almonds, pecans, peanuts, avocados, raisins, cinnamon, cloves, peppercorns, and chocolate. An ancient ceremonial dish, legend has it that Montezuma offered mole to the conquistadores of Spain, thinking them gods.

Nacho: An appetizer made from corn chips or tortillas broiled with cheese and jalapeño chiles or salsa on top.

Queso blanco: This is sold commercially as a substitute for Mexican cheese, which is a strong white cheese. Better substitutes, however, are either Monterey Jack cheese or ordinary farmer cheese to which salt and sour cream have been added for flavor.

Salsa rojo: Literally, "red sauce," salsa rojo is a puree made from serrano chiles and tomatoes. It is generally milder than salsa verde.

Salsa verde: Literally, "green sauce." It is made with similar ingredients to salsa rojo, but usually contains green chiles and fewer tomatoes, thus creating a sharper, more pungent sauce.

Sopaipillas: Originally a New Mexican recipe, this dessert is made from the same dough as wheat flour tortillas. Here, the dough is rolled thin, cut into small pieces, then fried until crisp and puffy. Sprinkled with cinnamon and powdered sugar, they are traditionally served cold in the evening with coffee.

Taco: A tortilla—either a soft tortilla, cooked but untoasted, or a hard one, toasted, roasted, or fried—wrapped around any number of fillings; usually tacos contain meat, chiles, shredded cheese, lettuce, and other vegetables.

Tamale: Cornmeal (masa) usually mixed with meat, chile, and sometimes herbs and then steamed in corn husks or banana leaves. There are, however, many different kinds of tamales—for example, sweet tamales can be made from masa, eggs, and butter with coconut, cream, jellies, or nuts.

Tortilla: The true "bread" of Mexico, tortillas are like corn crepes that serve as envelopes for nearly all Mexican food. These unleavened pancakes, made from dried, ground corn, are grilled lightly and served warm.

Tostada: An hors d'oeuvre made from toasted tortilla covered with beans, shredded cheese, meat, etc.

Index